USING **ADOBE**®
CONNECT

INSTRUCTOR-LED WORKBOOK

Todd McCall

e STRUCT

Using Adobe Connect

Credits

Author:
Todd McCall, Adobe Certified Expert / Instructor

Technical Contributor:
Jennifer Rossi, BBA

Copy Editor:
John Corrigan, BMath, MBA
Jason Holland BEd
Cara MacMullin BSc, N.D.
Chad Upton BA

Layout Designer:
Todd McCall, Adobe Certified Expert / Instructor

Welcome to Your eStruct Workbook

Thank you for choosing eStruct for your Adobe Connect training textbook. eStruct, a software instructional textbook firm established in 2015 to help simplify the software training process. At eStruct, we strive to provide thorough, current, and easy-to-follow instructions that allow you to quickly and effectively become a power user of Adobe Connect. At eStruct, we guarantee the quality of our textbooks. Every chapter and exercise was written by industry experts and thoroughly tested to insure quality education.

eStruct workbooks follow the simple philosophy: Start at the beginning, and build. With each chapter, you will continue to work through your Adobe Connect meeting room, all the way to a complete interactive and sophisticated meeting room. This process will help the beginner-meeting user, as well as help refresh any long-time Adobe Connect user.

Throughout Your eStruct Workbook You Will Find:

Time Required:
At the beginning of every chapter there will be an estimated time required to complete the chapter, this is a suggested time only.

Note:
Within each chapter you will find many Quick Tips, these are additional time-saving suggestions from industry professionals.

Note:
Throughout the chapters, there are small notes listed. These notes are small additional pieces of info that can help further understand that topic.

About the Author

Todd McCall is an official Adobe Certified Instructor and is an Adobe Certified Expert in Adobe Photoshop, Illustrator, Captivate, Presenter, Connect Meetings & Events and Adobe Connect Training. He has been teaching courses on the Adobe Enterprise eLearning suite since 2011, and is an industry expert on eLearning development. A former Publication Designer and Art Director, McCall began instructing at Durham College in the Advertising Program for the School of Media Art & Design just outside of Toronto, Ontario, Canada. In an effort to educate professionals on the use of eLearning authoring tools and webinar software, McCall began eStructing in 2015, a software instructional book company designed to help fill the void between online instruction and the software itself. Using Adobe Connect is his first book.

Chapter Index

Chapter Index

Chapter Index

Introduction to Web Conferencing and Adobe Connect

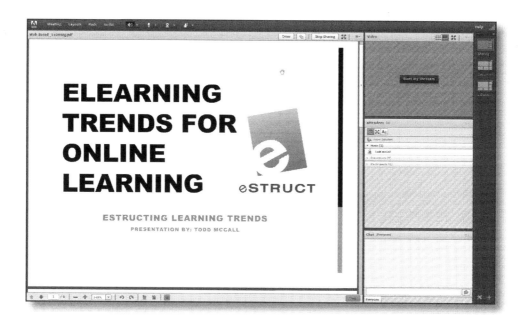

Adobe Connect, formerly Presedia Publishing system and Macromedia Breeze, is an interactive web conference system designed to share information and presentations among individuals or groups at multiple locations. Adobe Connect can also act as an on-demand learning management system, allowing learning managers or system administrators to create courses with self-directed presentations. Additionally, Adobe Connect also creates informative reports of detailed metrics including user quiz scores of on-demand training, meeting attendance and engagement time with meeting participants. For more information on Adobe Connect Reports, training and Advanced Administration features, be sure to explore 'Administrating Adobe Connect - Todd McCall' available in early 2017.

Adobe Connect typically is a 'Cloud' or 'Hosted' service, although it can be locally installed on individual servers. Being a 'Hosted' system, users can easily log into their account from any location, host a meeting, participate in webinars or complete a course. Adobe Connect is currently (October 2016) a Flash-based system that requires Adobe Flash Player to participate in a meeting, although some advanced features of Adobe Connect require the install of an Adobe Connect Add-In. (See page XIV for required software and Connect Add-In install).

Throughout this book, we will explore all that is needed to create and host meetings, and cover essential administration set-up for Adobe Connect Meetings. Adobe Connect is an easy-to-lean webinar solution and after completing this workbook you will have the skills to host and troubleshoot meetings of all sizes. For advanced instruction, see page 153 for additional training resources.

Creating a Trial Adobe Connect Account

For users looking to sample Adobe Connect and experience its web-conferencing software, Adobe offers a 30-day trial of Adobe Connect, with functionality capable of hosting up to 25 participants in meetings. To receive a trial Adobe Connect account, visit: http://www.adobe.com/products/adobeconnect.html.

How to set-up a trial:

1:   Click on 'Free Trial' in the top right corner.

The Adobe Connect landing page allows anyone to register for a free 30 day trial of Adobe Connect.

2:   Complete the required questions.

3:   Be sure to select 'Adobe Connect Meeting' when asked which solution you would like to try. For further information on Adobe Connect Learning, or Webinar, see page 153 for additional training resources.

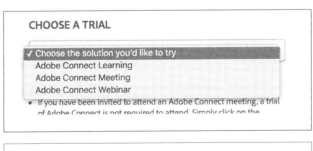

Be sure to choose the correct trial type.

This screen will indicate that your application was successfully submitted.

...npleting the trial request questionnaire, you will receive an email with a meeting web ...obe Connect account (also know as a 'URL') as well as your username and temporary

This is the email you will receive after you register for a free 30-day trial of Adobe Connect.

Required Software and the Adobe Connect Add-In

Adobe Connect is web-based software. To participate in a meeting, view presentations or interact via webcam or microphone use, Adobe Connect requires the Adobe Flash Player to be installed on your system. Typically this is already installed when using Google Chrome as an Internet browser. If an attendee does not have Adobe Flash Player installed, Adobe Connect will prompt the user to install the Adobe Connect Add-In (As of Adobe Connect 9.5.2.) If you want to install Flash Player before your first Adobe Connect experience, it is available for download at: https://get.adobe.com/flashplayer.

The Adobe Flash Player is a quick and easy application to install on your system.

Although Adobe Connect requires only Flash Player to begin, some features will remain restricted. If you want to share your screen during a software walk-through, for example, or utilize additional features, you will need to install the Adobe Connect Add-In. This software allows you to connect to a meeting independent of an Internet browser. It is recommended that all users install the Adobe Connect Add-In application for full meeting stability and functionality. To install the Add-In, visit: http://www.adobe.com/support/connect/downloads-updates.html Here you will see 'Download latest Adobe Connect 9 Meeting Add-In for Mac or PC.' Select your system and follow the install instructions. Be sure to restart your system after installing the Connect Add-In.

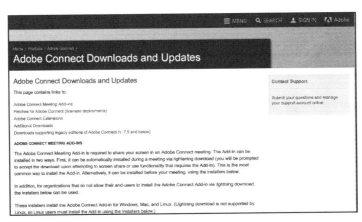

Be sure to check back for Adobe Connect Add-In Updates often.

NOTE: As Adobe Connect evolves and new features are added, your Adobe Connect account will attempt to update its Adobe Connect Add-In. Please be aware of this, especially if your system is company-issued and requires administration access to install updates. Please test your system prior to your meeting to avoid any delays or disruptions.

If you want to send a diagnostic connection test to a meeting participant, Adobe offers a connection test page that has links to Adobe Flash and the Adobe Connect Add-In installer. Keep this URL handy: http://admin.adobeconnect.com/common/help/en/support/meeting_test.htm or Google 'Adobe Connect Connection Test.' The link will test your system and recommend any additional software installations.

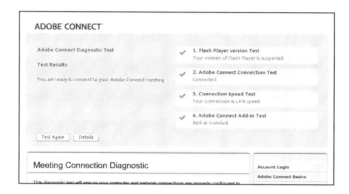

The Adobe Connect Connection test page will analyze your system and report any challenges you may have.

Because Adobe Connect is Flash-based, certain functions require a mouse. This prevents tablets and mobile devices from connecting to a meeting. To allow these users to participate, Adobe Connect has a mobile application which connects users to meetings independently. This free and convenient application will allow tablet and mobile device users to have meeting functionality with the exception of just a few features.

The Adobe Connect App is a simple solution to access, host and participate in meeting remotely through a tablet of mobile device.

For a complete listing of the Adobe Connect technical requirements please visit https://helpx.adobe.com/adobe-connect/tech-specs.html

Adobe Connect Central

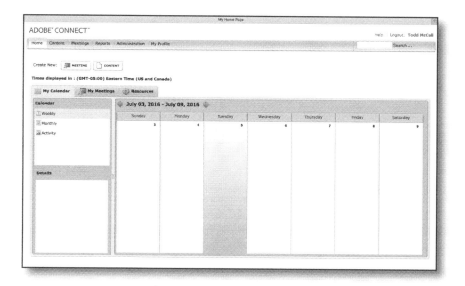

Overview:

Throughout this chapter we will explore Adobe Connect Central and its various tabs and features, along with the adjustments contained within each.

In This Chapter:

Time Required:
This chapter should take 30 minutes to explore all the features of Adobe Connect Central.

Once you have your account login information, you will need to start in the administrative portal (the 'back end') of Adobe Connect - Adobe Connect Central, it's basically the Grand Central Station of your Adobe Connect account. As a System Administrator this is where all the magic happens. Here you will create meetings, add users, send meeting invites, upload and organize content, manage meeting recordings and download meeting reports.

In the welcome email you receive after setting up your account, you will notice your account URL. Select this is a direct link to your Adobe Connect Central, this URL will be used often so please bookmark it. If you have purchased an account, you can request a custom URL.

Custom URL Example: mycompany.adobeconnect.com.

Note:
Be sure to check your spam or junk folder for your trial account confirmation.

Your Adobe Connect trial registration will include your Adobe Connect URL as well as your user-name and password.

When you first visit your Adobe Connect Central URL, you will be asked to change your password.

Adobe Connect Central Landing Page

When you have successfully logged into your new Adobe Connect account you will see the Adobe Connect Central welcome screen. Here you will see several options including buttons to create 'Content' and 'Meetings'. The 'My Calendar' tab shows a list of weekly and monthly meeting rooms that are scheduled. 'My Meetings' shows a running list of meetings you have participated in, information about each meeting room and a calendar of your meetings.

Quick Tip:
If you are a meeting host or connect system administrator, you will have the option to create meetings or content right from the central landing page.

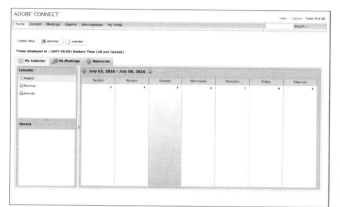

The Adobe Connect Landing page will show you a simple listing of events for which you are registered.

Adobe Connect Central Tab Menu

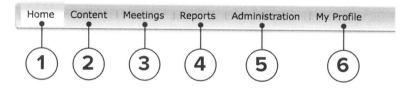

Note:
The Tab bar in Adobe Connect Central can vary based on the account type you have, ex. If you have a 'Learning' account you will have a 'Training' Tab.

1: Home

The Adobe Connect Central 'Home' Tab is also the Adobe Connect Central landing page. This page shows a list of all meetings, training, and events for which you are registered. You can view your registered items in a list view, or calendar view (by week or month).

2: Content

The Content tab allows you to pre-upload any presentations, images or other useful files you might need for various meetings. Here you can organize all your files and easily load them into meetings. Managing your meeting content is further discussed in Chapter 16 - Managing Your Content.

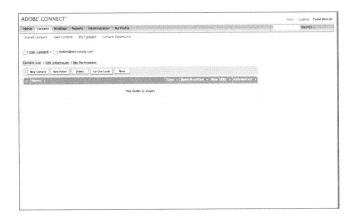

3: Meetings

The Meetings tab is where you create, modify, and organize meetings. As an administrator you can access meetings created by any user both in the user's folder and the shared meetings folder. Creation of Adobe Connect meetings is covered in detail in Chapter 3 - Creating an Adobe Connect Meeting Room.

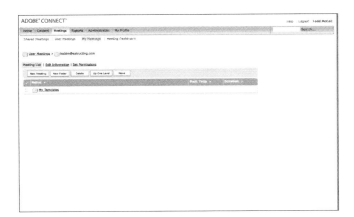

4: Reports

After a Meeting, Training or Adobe Connect Event, Adobe Connect Administrators can run various reports to get insight on user attendance, content usage, and post meeting metrics such as engagement. Meeting Reports are covered in the advanced Adobe Connect book: Administrating Adobe Connect - Todd McCall, January 2017.

Quick Tip:
Individual meeting reports are also available in the Meeting tab after a meeting has run.

5: Administration

In the Administration tab, you can: add/delete system users, create groups, view system usage, and customize your Adobe Connect account with logos, colors, and other options. The administration tab is only accessible to the Adobe Connect Central Administrator (If you just created your free trial, or purchased your account, you will likely be the system Administrator). An overview of Adobe Connect Administration is further covered in Chapter 2 - Basic Adobe Connect Administration. For Advanced Adobe Connect Administration, explore the continuation of this book: Administrating Adobe Connect - Todd McCall, available January, 2017.

Note:
The Adobe Connect Administration Tab is only accessible to connect system administrators. Creators of any Adobe Connect account are the system administrator by default.

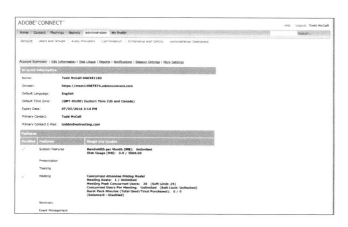

6: My Profile

Inside the Adobe Connect 'My Profile' tab, accessible to all users, you can reset passwords, update personal info and contact info. You can also view your group memberships and view your audio profiles and preferences.

CHAPTER NOTES

CHAPTER NOTES

Basic Adobe Connect Administration

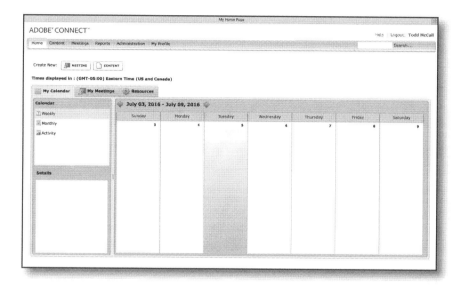

Overview:

Throughout this chapter, we will explore the Adobe Connect Administration tab. Some of the functions of it include: the creation of new users and groups, resetting passwords, and understanding the different roles that users can be assigned in the Adobe Connect system.

Time Required:
This chapter should take 30 minutes to explore all the features of the Adobe Connect Central.

In This Chapter:

System Users:

Inside Adobe Connect Central, navigate to the Administration tab, and select 'Users and Groups' submenu.

Inside the Users and Groups submenu, you will see a complete listing of all users 🔲 added to your Adobe Connect system. If this is your first time in your new or trial account, you should only have one user. This sole user should be yourself, and by default you will be the main system administrator.

Every user added to the system, regardless of their role in the system, is technically a system user. Users can be added to system groups to assign permissions to that user and they can be added to custom groups to make it easier to manage multiple users at the same time.

Default System Groups:

The Users and Groups panel will (depending on the type of account being used) show 4 groups 🔲 :

🔲 Administrators:

This group is for System Administrators and note that Adobe Connect systems can have an unlimited amount of system Administrators. System Administrators have complete control over the Adobe Connect system. Users who are added to this group can customize the entire system, add and delete users, content, and meetings.

🖾 Limited Administrators:

Limited Administrators can create meetings, manage content, and assign users to meetings but are not allowed to perform any of the Administrator rights such as creating, modifying or deleting users and groups, and adjusting any system customizations such as logos, background colors etc. For Advanced Adobe Connect Administration, explore the continuation of this book: Administrating Adobe Connect - Todd McCall, January 2017.

🖾 Meeting Hosts:

The meeting hosts group is the most important group, these group members essentially have the 'keys to the car.' They can turn meetings on and receive their own folders to store content and meetings. Users MUST belong to the meeting host group to start a meeting. Your system (if trial) will have one license, meaning your meeting hosts group can only contain one system user. This is how Adobe moderates your license.

🖾 Authors:

If you are creating content via an Adobe authoring tool such as Adobe Captivate or Adobe Presenter, you can publish your content directly to your Adobe Connect system. To do this, you must be a member of the authors group. if you purchase a full license, let the sales representative know you would like this functionality so they can set up your system with the right licenses.

Note:
If you have selected a different trial Ex. Adobe Connect Learning or Adobe Connect Webinar, you will have different or additional System Groups.

Creating Users

To create a new user on the system, select 'New User' from the bottom of the Users and Groups panel.

The new user creation page will appear. Complete the form using the following information to create a generic user (unless you have a specific person you can use for testing):

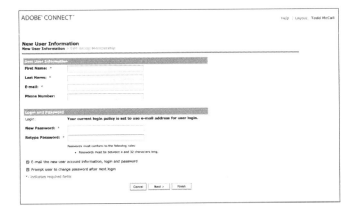

First Name: John
Last Name: Doe
Email: John.Doe@email.com
Phone Number: Optional
New Password: Password1234
Retype Password: Password1234
if you do this exercise, you will set up a new user and we can delete this user later.

Note:
You can have as many system users on your account as you want, there is no limit to the amount of users your account can have.

When creating a new user you have the option to select, 'Email the new user their account information, login and password.' For this example, we used a made-up email, so be sure this option is not selected so an email will not be sent.

By default Adobe Connect will also select 'Prompt user to change password after next login,' if you do not want the user to modify their password, you can deselect this.

After creating this new user, Adobe Connect will prompt you to select a group to which you will add this new user. Select 'Administrators' and select 'Add' below. After the membership is added select 'Finish.'

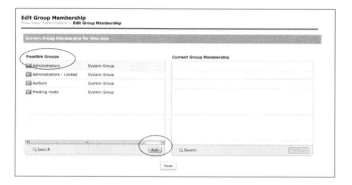

You will now see an overview of this user and can make any changes if needed.

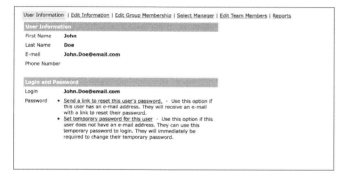

Creating Groups

To help keep your users organized, or add users to meeting in bulk, Adobe Connect administrators can create 'Groups.' To create a new user, select the User and Group panel submenu from the Administration tab, then select 'New Group.'

Quick Tip:
You can have groups inside of groups. For example, in larger Adobe Connect accounts you can create a group called 'Managers' and place that group in the administration and meeting host system group. In this situation you can easily just update your 'Managers' group members.

The 'New Group Information' dialog box will open. Enter 'My Students' as the name and enter a brief description of your choice. For example, 'This is a group for all our future meeting participants.'

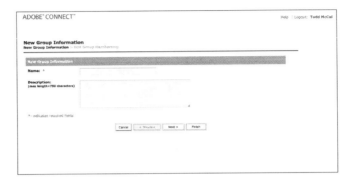

After creating your group, Adobe Connect Central will ask you to add users to this group. You can add users here directly from the list, or select finish to ignore, as we will cover adding users to a group next.

You will now have 'System Groups' and 'Administrator Groups.' Any group you create will be added as an 'Administrator Group.'

Note:

Any user added to a group will be given the same permissions as any 'System Group' under which that group is currently listed. For example, if you add a new user to your 'Manager' group and that manager group is added to the 'Administrators' group, then that user will now have administrative controls.

The primary feature to having administrator groups is after adding a group to a meeting, or multiple meetings. With a group that has been added to multiple meeting rooms, users can be quickly removed from multiple meetings at once by simply removing the user from the group. Additionally, multiple users can be quickly added to meetings by simply adding the group instead of adding individual users one at a time.

Adding / Removing Users from Groups

Once a group is created, you can always go back and edit the group membership. To do so, select the Administration tab inside Adobe Connect Central and then select the 'Users and Groups.' Highlight the 'My Students' group we created earlier by selecting it once and then click the 'Information' button.

Quick Tip:
You can also import a list of users via CSV file and add them directly to groups with one simple action. This is further covered in the "Administrating Adobe Connect - Todd McCall, January 2017" eStruct book.

Select 'View Group Members.'

You can now add or remove any user from this group by selecting the user from the possible group members and then selecting 'Add,' or selecting the user from the 'Current Group Members' and selecting 'Remove.' To try this, select John Doe and 'Add' this user to the group, then 'Remove' this user.

Deleting Users and Groups

Be sure to keep your Adobe Connect system up-to-date with your user list by deleting unwanted users and groups. To do so, select the Administration tab inside Adobe Connect Central then select the 'Users and Groups' submenu if you are not already inside this panel. To delete a user or group, select the user or group in the Users and Group list, then select 'Delete.' To practice this, delete the Group 'My Students' and then delete 'John Doe' -- the user you created earlier. If you started with a new or trial account of Adobe Connect, your Users and Groups list will now only contain your system groups and yourself.

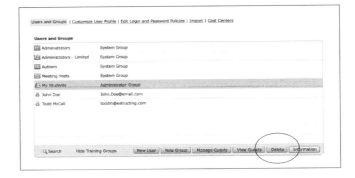

Resetting Users Passwords

From time to time a user might lose or forget their password. As the system administrator, it will be your job to manage this problem. Fortunately, Adobe Connect makes it very easy to reset passwords. To edit passwords, select the Administration tab inside Adobe Connect Central and then select the 'Users and Groups' submenu if you are not already inside this panel. Select the user then select 'Information.'

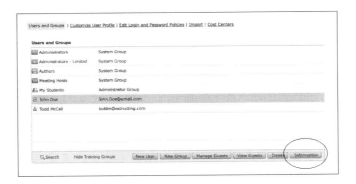

Note:
Deleting user groups will not delete the group members from the system, you must delete individual users one user at a time.

The Information page for the select user will appear.

User Information | Edit Information | Edit Group Membership | Select Manager | Edit Team Members | Reports

User Information

First Name   **John**
Last Name   **Doe**
E-mail   **John.Doe@email.com**
Phone Number

Login and Password

Login   **John.Doe@email.com**
Password   • Send a link to reset this user's password. - Use this option if
               this user has an e-mail address. They will receive an e-mail
               with a link to reset their password.
             • Set temporary password for this user - Use this option if this
               user does not have an e-mail address. They can use this
               temporary password to login. They will immediately be
               required to change their temporary password.

*Adobe Connect user
information overview.*

Quick Tip:
Users who log into Adobe Connect Central can also update their password by selecting the 'My Profile' tab and then selecting 'Change My Password.'

When resetting a password you can either send a link to reset the user's password which is a quick way to send the user their current password, or setting a temporary password for this user. This option is typically a very fast option as you can tell the user their new temporary password with which they can login before they are immediately prompted to set a new password of their choice.

CHAPTER NOTES

Creating a Meeting Room

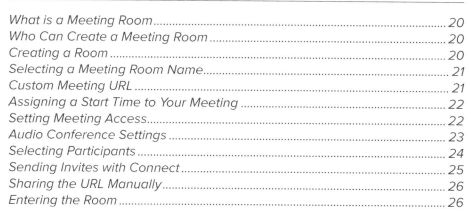

Overview:

Throughout this chapter, we will explore the creation and management of Adobe Connect meeting rooms. This includes the various meeting room preferences, meeting start times, adding participants and inviting participants to meetings by sharing the meeting room URL.

Time Required:
This chapter should take 45 minutes to explore all the aspects of creating an Adobe Connect Meeting Room.

In This Chapter:

What is a Meeting Room

Adobe Connect meeting rooms are essentially virtual gathering places such as virtual classrooms and conference rooms. Users can all view the same screen, hear each other with their computer's microphone and speakers (or headphones), see each other with their web cameras, share documents, post web links, interact with questions or create a private queue of questions for a guest lecturer or speaker.

Adobe Connect meeting rooms are persistent, that means they do not disappear after the meeting is over, they can be re-used time and time again. This is advantageous because all of the settings you change and all of the content you load into the meeting room will be retained for future meetings, reducing setup time in the future.

Each time a room is used, that use is referred to as a 'Session' of that meeting room. Although every meeting room starts out the same, there are many options you can customize when initially creating the room. Throughout this chapter we will explore the creation of a meeting room and all the available options when creating a meeting room.

Who Can Create a Meeting Room

To create an Adobe Connect meeting room, a user must be a member of at least one of the following built-in user groups: Administrator, Limited System Administrator or Meeting Host. Without a membership to any of these groups, you will not have a 'Meeting' tab to access the 'New Meeting' feature in Adobe Connect Central.

Please refer to Chapter 1 to explore the various tabs inside Adobe Connect Central and Chapter 2 to review how to add / remove users from groups.

Creating a Room

Once inside the Adobe Connect Central, select the 'Meetings' tab.

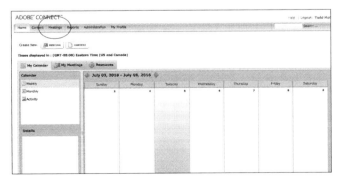

Click the 'New Meeting' button just above the meeting room list. If this is your first time creating a meeting, your 'Meeting List' will be empty.

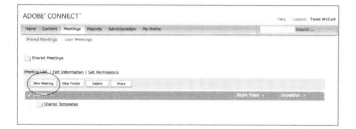

Quick Tip:
Meeting hosts have a quick link to create a meeting room on the landing page of Adobe Connect Central.

The following steps show you how to customize your new Adobe Connect meeting room.

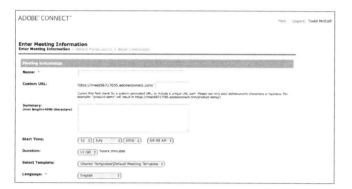

Selecting a Meeting Room Name

You can give your meeting room any name you want and you are allowed to have meeting room name duplicates as meeting room names might also be used by other instructors. For our exercise, enter 'New Employee Training' in the 'Name' field; this name can be changed later.

Custom Meeting URL

By default, if you leave the custom URL blank, Adobe Connect will assign a unique URL such as 'r1jby5eqfik.' Although this is quick and convenient to create, this can get confusing for you and your students if you manually distribute the URL to invite participants. To make your experience easier, Adobe Connect allows you to assign a custom URL.

All meeting room URLs will be an extension of your Adobe Connect Central URL, for example: https://mycompany.adobeconnect.com/r1jby5eqfik/ For this exercise, enter 'NEWEMPLOYEE' as the custom URL.

You can add a brief (4000 character max) summary for your meeting. This summary will be included when you send out email invites to attendees who are invited to the meeting. For this example enter, 'Meeting room for all new employee training.'

Assigning a Start Time to Your Meeting

Keep in mind that meeting rooms are persistent. Meeting rooms 'open' when the meeting host enters the meeting room. The host also has controls to end and restart meeting rooms. As a guideline, Adobe Connect allows you to assign a meeting 'Start Time' and 'Duration.' This will be referenced in your meeting room invites and on the meeting room list and calendar of the Adobe Connect Central for all registered attendees. This start time and duration can be changed at any time, so it is only important as a reference for all attendees but has no effect on the actual start time and end time of the meeting.

For this example, select a start time two days from now, beginning at 10:00am. Assign the meeting room a duration of 2 hours.

Leave the 'Select Template' as the 'Default Meeting Template' and 'English' if this is the preferred language for your meeting.

Note:
You can customize meeting room templates and use these meeting rooms as templates for future meetings. This is explored in detail in the 'Administrating Adobe Connect - Todd McCall, January 2017' Book.

Setting Meeting Access

When initially creating your meeting you will need to set the meeting access. There are 3 possible access types:

1:   Only registered users may enter the room (guest access is blocked).

If you are having a private or confidential meeting, you would only want registered guests to be able to access the meeting room, and therefore the meeting landing page would not have an option for guests to enter. This option requires that all attendees are set up with a username and password.

2: Only registered users and accepted guests may enter the room.

If you are flexible with your meeting room attendees you can set your meeting to allow registered users and 'accepted' guests into the meeting room. If you select as an access type "Accepted Guests", then this will allow a non-registered participant, who had the meeting room URL, to request access to the meeting room by simply entering their name and requesting access. As the meeting host, you will receive a notification in the meeting room that this attendee would like to access the meeting and you can approve or decline their request. This calls for more work when in the meeting room for the host, but allows complete control over the meeting room attendees.

3:   Anyone who has the URL for the meeting can enter the room.

If you are having a public webinar or public meeting where you will be sharing non-confidential information, this is the access type you would select. This creates less work for the meeting host, but offers no security for who might enter your meeting room. However, this access option still requires that attendees enter a name before entering.

For this exercise, choose the default option: 'Only registered users and accepted guests may enter the room.'

Audio Conference Settings

When setting up your Adobe Connect meeting it is important to think about how you want to communicate with your audience. There are 3 Audio Conference Settings:

1:   Do not include any audio conference with this meeting.

If you are using the in-meeting audio, 'Voice over Internet Protocol' or VOIP' you will selection this option since you are not using a teleconferencing solution.

Quick Tip:
When in a meeting, you can block guest access temporarily, to make a meeting private from guests.

Note:
When you run your first meeting and you are unaware of your users system including microphones and speakers, it could be easier to use an audio conference provider (not included in the trial.)

2:   Include this audio conference with this meeting.

You can choose to have you an audio conference line (not part of Adobe Connect) integrated with your meeting room, this is referred to as an audio bridge and explained in detail in the 'Administrating Adobe Connect' Book.

3:   Include other audio conference with this meeting.

If you want to use an external audio conference system to broadcast your audio, you can include the conference information and this will be included on the meeting room invites. This is a simple solution when you have attendees without speaker or microphones.

For this example we will choose 'Do not include any audio conference with this meeting' and then select 'Next.'

Selecting Participants

Once you have completed the initial settings for your meeting room, Adobe Connect will ask you to select participants for your meeting room. You can add up to 25 participants with a trial account, or up to 100 if you have a licensed account. For meeting rooms exceeding 100 attendees, please contact your Adobe Connect sales representative.

Quick Tip:
When in a meeting, you can change the meeting room role for any attendee from 'Participant' to 'Presenter' to 'Host' easily.

To add participants, simply select the user, and then select 'Add.' You can also select a role for this new participant. When you assign a role to an attendee, that attendee will have different rights in the meeting room such as microphone access, or document sharing. Meeting roles are explained in detail on page 43.

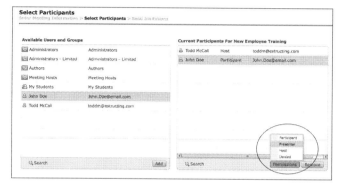

Quick Tip:
If you will be posting your meeting room URL on a public page and not using Invites, you can select 'Finish' to ignore the invite page, and quickly copy the meeting room URL.

Once you have selected all your meeting room participants, select 'Next' to access the meeting room invitations.

Sending Invitations with Connect

After selecting meeting room participants, you can send out invitations to all the meeting room attendees via email. If you decide to send out invitations, you can customize who will receive the email invitations and also customize what the email will contain. By default the email will contain the Name, Summary, Start Time, URL, and a quick link to run a Meeting Room Connection Diagnostic.

Adobe Connect meeting room invitation set-up.

Quick Tip:
Asking your attendees to run the diagnostic prior to entering their first meeting may help prevent any delays starting your meeting.

For this exercise, send invitations to the meeting host only (yourself) and do not modify the email. This will ensure you receive a sample of the default meeting room invite. Then select 'Finish' to complete the meeting setup.

Adobe Connect Meeting Room Sample invitation email.

Sharing the URL Manually

Once you have completed the meeting room setup, you will be taken to the meeting room information summary page.

Quick Tip:
When in a meeting room, you can quickly select 'Invite Participants' if you forgot to add someone to the meeting and/or want to email the URL to a potential Attendee.

Here, you will see all the settings you have selected for this meeting room, including the meeting room URL. If you choose to manually email the URL to attendees, you can copy this URL and paste it directly into an email or calendar invite.

Entering the Room

On the meeting Information information summary page, you will see a quick link to enter the meeting room. Select 'Enter Meeting Room' and the meeting room will open in a new window.

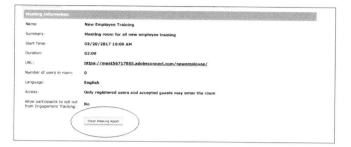

Quick Tip:
Bookmark your meeting room URLs for easy access to rooms you use regular. This link will give you the ability to enter your room as a host by entering your credentials without first navigating to Adobe Connect Central.

CHAPTER NOTES

_____

_____

_____

_____

_____

_____

_____

_____

_____

_____

_____

_____

_____

_____

_____

Meeting Features

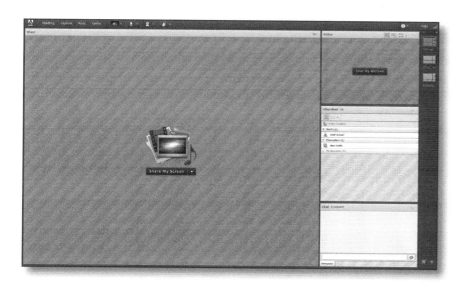

Overview:

Throughout this chapter, we will explore the Adobe Connect meeting interface, all the menus and how to access various meeting features.

In This Chapter:

Time Required:
This chapter should take 20 minutes to cover the features of an Adobe Connect meeting room

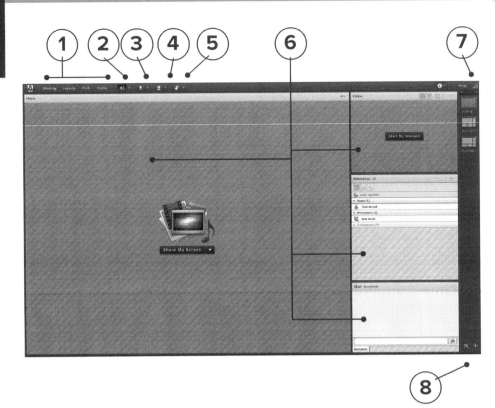

1: Meeting Drop Down Menus

The Adobe Connect meeting drop down menus allow you access to various features. Throughout this book the various 'drop down menus' will be referenced.

2: Speaker Volume

Meeting attendees can adjust their speaker volume or mute their meeting audio with the speaker volume button.

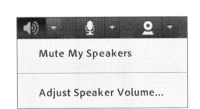

3: Connect My Audio

Chapter 8 covers the various options when connecting your meeting audio, selecting and calibrating your microphone as well as muting your microphone.

4: Start My Webcam

Chapter 9 covers the various options when connecting, and broadcasting your camera.

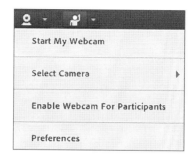

5: Set Status

Chapter 5 covers the 'Set Status' feature, which allows meeting participants to silently interact with the meeting host and participants by selecting a meeting status.

Quick Tip:
The menu in the top right corner of most pods opens the 'Pod Options' for that type of pod. In here you can access a variety of custom features.

6: Meeting Pods

Every Adobe Connect meeting room is a collection of pods. Think of a pod as a window or an app -- different pods can perform different functions. For example the Share pod allows you to upload and display documents for other people to see, while the Video pod allows you to share a webcam stream.

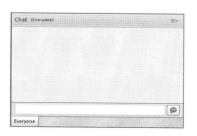

4

7: Connection Status

In the top right corner of every Adobe Connect meeting room is a small signal strength icon similar to a cell phone service icon. This is where you access the Connection Status panel. In the event of a connection issue, this indicates the strength of your internet connection to Adobe Connect.

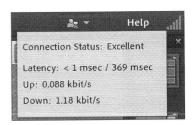

8: Layout Bar

The default Adobe Connect meeting room templates include three customizable layouts, you can add more layouts quickly by clicking on the '+' icon at the bottom of the layout panel. In the 'Administrating Adobe Connect - Todd McCall, January 2017' Book, we discuss creating custom layouts.

CHAPTER NOTES

CHAPTER NOTES

Meeting Attendees

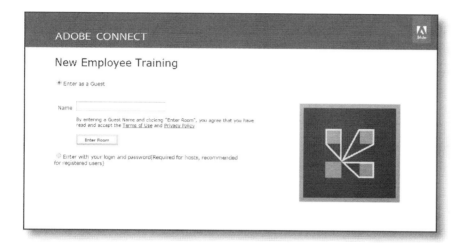

Chapter 5

Overview:

Throughout this chapter, we explore how guests and registered users access the meeting room, how to place Participants on hold while you prepare your meeting and how to prevent users from accessing the meeting after it has begun.

Time Required:
This chapter should take 30 minutes to explore all the aspects of Adobe Connect meeting room attendees.

In This Chapter:

Meeting Attendees

The meeting becomes up and running when the 'Meeting Host 'logs into the meeting room. This can only happen if the user role is set as 'Host' for that particular meeting (covered in chapter 3) and the user is a member of the 'Meeting Hosts' system user group (Covered in chapter 2). Now that your meeting is officially up and running, we need to allow in participants and set up some in-meeting preferences to help organize and moderate your meeting.

Welcoming Accepted Guests

As attendees connect to the meeting room, they will be greeted with a login page. If they are a 'Registered Guest' they will enter their email and password as originally set when they were added to the Adobe Connect system; if they are not registered to the meeting, and are not a registered user to your Adobe Connect System, they will have the option to enter as an guest by simply typing in their name and requesting entry. However, if the meeting access was set to the first option, 'Only registered users,' the 'Enter as a Guest' option will not be available.

Quick Tip:
The logo on the welcome page is customizable and found in the administration tab 'Customize.'

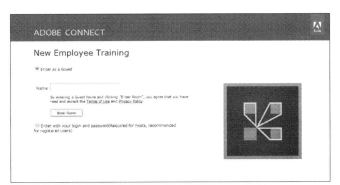

Adobe Connect meeting room landing page.

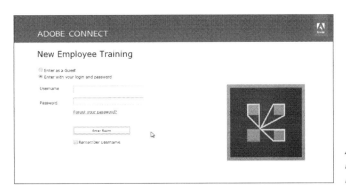

Adobe Connect meeting room registered user login.

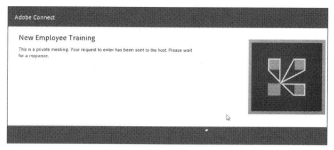

Adobe Connect landing page after requesting guest entry to a meeting room, waiting for access.

As a meeting host, when inside the room, you will be notified when guests try to access the meeting. You have the ability to accept or decline these users. Additionally, you can let all requests collect in a list and accept all requests at once. New requests after that can be treated the same way.

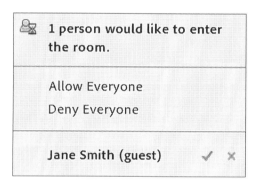

Requested access notification for meeting hosts.

Quick Tip:
When 2 or more guests request access to a meeting room a list of meeting entry requests will build, by selecting 'Allow Everyone' all requests to enter are accepted at once.

Inviting Attendees

If you accidentally forgot to invite an attendee, or they have misplaced their invite URL, you can quickly send an invitation to that user. To invite an attendee in a meeting, select 'Manage Access and Entry' from the Meeting drop down menu, then select 'Invite Participants.'

Adobe Connect 'Manage Access and Entry' menu.

Quick Tip:
When clicking 'Manage Meeting Information,' Adobe Connect will open a browser window and take you to the meeting information page of this meeting inside Adobe Connect Central.

Meeting Attendees

This will open a window where you can either copy the meeting URL or select 'Compose e-mail' which will create a draft email invite using your default mail client. You can then send this meeting URL to anyone.

Blocking Access to the Meeting

Once your meeting is up and running you can avoid any interruptions of late-coming attendees or guests. In the meeting access menu select 'Block Guest Access,' this will not allow any guests to request entry to the meeting.

Note:
Licensed meetings have a capacity of 100, once you get close to that capacity you can block guest access to avoid a meeting from reaching it's capacity.

If you select 'Block Incoming Attendees...' you can prevent any users from entering the meeting. This would likely be used if you were having a very confidential meeting and did not want anyone else to enter the meeting. Be aware that if a participant losses their meeting connection, this feature will prevent them from re-entering the meeting room.

When blocking incoming attendee access to your meeting, Adobe Connect will ask you to provide a notification message for the users explaining why they are blocked from the meeting. You can customize this to say anything you may want your attendees to know. For example "Unfortunately you cannot access this meeting as it is already in progress"

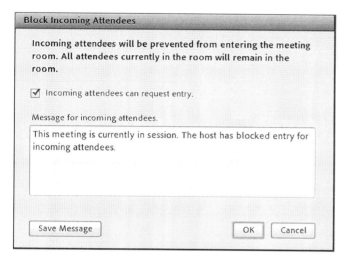

Quick Tip:
When you block incoming Attendees, the information panel will allow you to change the message you post for incoming attendees.

Placing Participants on Hold

During a meeting you may want to prevent participants from viewing your meeting while you prepare your presentation or load documents. Selecting 'Placing Participants On Hold' will show a blank screen to the participants explaining what is happening. This notification is customizable.

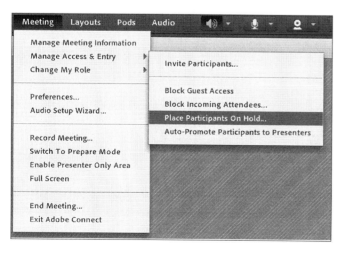

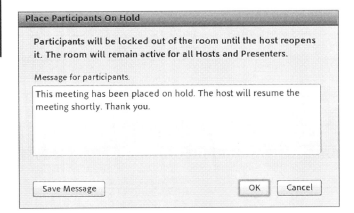

Adobe Connect Notifications

Once you place a meeting on hold, or block incoming guest access, Adobe Connect will show a meeting notification to the meeting host. This notification center will show all the custom features currently set for the current meeting room. From this notification drop down you can turn off these custom features.

Adobe Connect drop down notification center.

Participant Status

When an attendee enters a room, their role will determine the meeting room features they can access, and by default all accepted guests will enter a meeting room as a 'Participant.' participants must be granted access to meeting room features such as microphone rights or web-cam rights, until then, all participants can interact with the meeting room via 'Participant Status.'

As a participant, you can set and clear your status. This status is an easy way to communicate with the entire meeting.

Quick Tip:
Many educators use the 'Agree' feature to ask their audience questions.

Once a participant changes their status, an icon will appear beside their name in the Attendee pod.

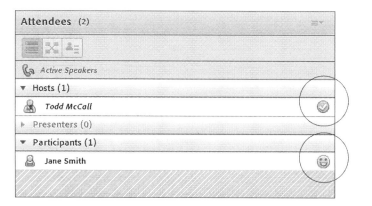

Quick Tip:
When you click on the Attendee pod option icon in the top right corner of the Attendee pod, you can select 'Clear Everyone's Status' to quickly reset the custom status of all attendees.

Often attendees will use this feature to tell the presenter if they need the presenter to speak louder, softer, or to adjust the speed of their presentation. If an attendee needs to step away from the meeting they can select 'Step Away' this will send a pop-up notification to the meeting host.

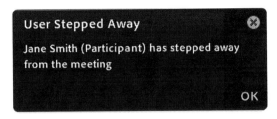

User Stepped Away

Jane Smith (Participant) has stepped away from the meeting

OK

User stepped away notification the meeting host will receive.

Note:
As users step away the meeting host will see a notification indicating who has stepped away, this will disappear on it's own. The raised hand notification will not disappear until the host accepts or closes the notification.

An additional feature in the status menu is the "Raise Hand" feature. This allows you to send a notification to the meeting host and is a great way for participants to notify the host that they have a question or concern. The meeting host can choose to accept or ignore your raised hand.

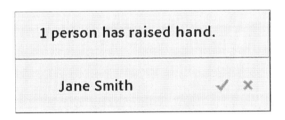

1 person has raised hand.

Jane Smith ✓ ✗

Notification the meeting host will receive when an attendee has set the raise hand status.

Registered Users Vs. Guests

When first creating a meeting you can assign roles to registered users. Each role will allow that user to have access to certain meeting features.

By default the meeting creator will be added to the meeting as a 'Host' and have full access to the meeting room features. Registered attendees will be added as 'Participants' although you can set these users with different roles, for example you can have certain registered guests set as presenters if you know they will be sharing any documents. When an accepted guest enters the room they are set as a participant, this role can be changed by the meeting host at any time.

Meeting Attendee Roles:

The following are the three types of users and the features these roles can access.

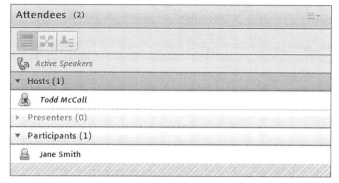

Attendee pod shown with 2 attendees. The italic name will always identify yourself.

Note:
As the original meeting host you can promote and demote yourself.

Participants

Participants have very little access to features by default. They can set their status, type in the Chat pods, respond to polls, raise their hand and once web-cam or microphone rights have been granted by the meeting host, they will have access to these additional features.

Presenters

When a participant is promoted to a presenter they can share documents, presentations, turn on their microphone and web-cam, adjust meeting pod size, and location but they are restricted from adjusting any of the meeting preferences or changing between layouts.

Quick Tip:
When you select the Attendee pod options in the top right corner of the Attendee pod, you can select 'Edit my info' and change your name. All attendees can access this feature.

Hosts

A meeting host essentially has full access to all the meeting features, they can promote /demote other users, allow guests to enter the meeting, invite participants, record the meeting, turn on and share web-cams, microphones, or presentations. Additionally meeting hosts can initiate breakout rooms, modify the meeting room layout, adjust meeting preferences and create new meeting room pods. Hosts also have the ability to remove people from the meeting room if required.

Promote / Demote Attendees

All meeting hosts have the ability to promote / demote all attendees. To give a participant presenter rights, simply click-hold-and-drag that attendee's name from the participant to the presenter list in the attendee panel. You can easily move that same attendee back to a participant the same way. Additionally, as a host, if you mouse-over any attendee's name in the attendee list, a panel of options will appear including 'Make Presenter,' clicking this option also promotes that attendee.

Note:
There is no limit to the amount of meeting hosts or presenters you can have inside the meeting, the only restriction is the total room occupancy.

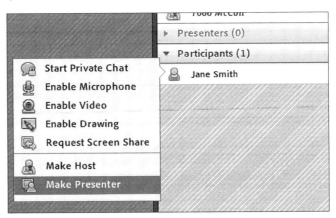

Auto Promoting Participants

Occasionally you may have a meeting where you want all participants to become presenters, typically because this is the fastest way to allow all attendees to have sharing and microphone rights. In the Meeting drop down menu, inside the 'Manage Access & Entry' section, select 'Auto-Promote Participants to Presenters.' This feature will also appear in the Adobe Connect notifications panel.

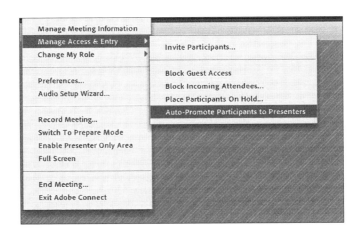

CHAPTER NOTES

Chat Pod

Overview:

Throughout this chapter, we will explore the features and functionality of the Chat pod. We will also customize the Chat pod, its preferences and explore private chatting.

In This Chapter:

Time Required:
This chapter should take 30 minutes to explore all the aspects of the Adobe Connect Chat pod.

The Chat Pod

The Chat pod allows users without microphone access to message others in the meeting, ask questions, or provide general feedback to all meeting attendees. Any message typed into the Chat pod will be visible for all attendees when the Chat pod is visible. You can customize many aspects of how your chat transcript appears and how message notifications appear to the host. Additionally, meeting attendees can send private messages directly to other attendees.

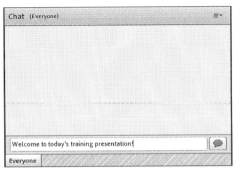

Adobe Connect Chat pod.

Note:

All Adobe Connect meeting rooms can have multiple Chat pods, for further info, refer to chapter 11.

Your Chat Text Size

All attendees have the ability to adjust the font size of their Chat pod. This makes the pod more functional to all Attendees as some may have a preference for larger fonts. To adjust your font size, select 'Text Size' from the Chat pod options panel icon located in the top right corner of the Chat pod, then scroll down to select your desired font size. A dot will appear beside the current font size. This new font size will display for your meeting experience only and not change for any other attendees.

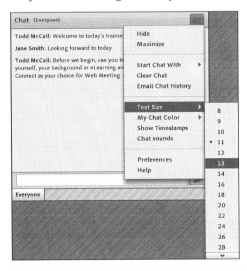

Chat type size can be customized to any size.

Your Chat Color

As the chat transcript grows, or as more attendees are chatting, it may be easier for you to identify your messages by changing your chat color. This will change for all your messages in the Chat pod and also appear in a custom color for all attendees. To change your chat color, select 'My Chat Color' from the Chat pod options icon in the top right corner of the Chat pod, then select a custom color. A dot will appear beside the current chat color.

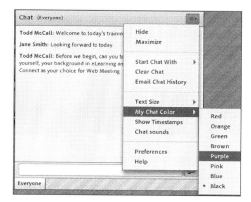

Adobe Connect Chat pod text color options.

Private Messages

Throughout a meeting you may want to chat privately with a specific participant and prevent other attendees from seeing that message. To start a private chat, move your cursor over an attendees name in the Attendee pod, a pop-up will appear where you can select 'Start Private Chat.' Once you select this option, a tab with that chosen attendee's name will appear in your Chat pod. Select this tab and begin typing your private message. For example, presenters often chat with each other discussing items or topics to discuss during a presentation or webinar.

Quick Tip:
When private messages are started, only the sender and recipient will have access to those messages.

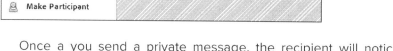

Once a you send a private message, the recipient will notice a yellow flashing tab appear in their Chat pod indicating there is a new private message.

Chat Pod

Once the recipient selects the private message tab they can begin having a private conversation. Private messaging cannot be exported or seen by any other attendee.

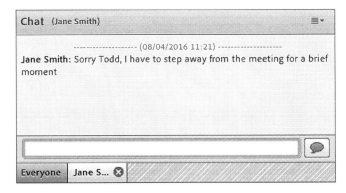

Adobe Connect Chat pod with private messages.

Disabling Private Chat

Private chatting can often distract your audience, as they can get side tracked with other conversations. As a meeting host you can disable the private messaging to avoid any distraction from your audience. To disable the private chatting, select 'Preferences' from the Chat pod options panel icon located in the top right corner of the Chat pod, this will open the Chat pod section of the meeting preferences panel. This can also be accessed by selecting 'Preferences' from the Meeting drop down menu the top of the meeting room.

Once you have the Chat pod preferences open, deselect the option for 'Enable Private Chat for Participants.' If Attendees are already in a private chat they will get a notification in that private chat tab that private chatting has been disabled.

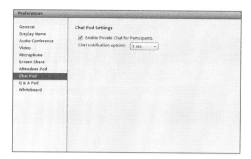

Chat Timestamps

Quick Tip:
Always reference the timestamps when responding to any questions posted in the Chat pod to avoid answering the same question twice.

As the meeting progresses you may receive questions from attendees and to make sure you see them, you have the option to turn on timestamps. A timestamp will list the time each message was received, helping you keep track of new messages or questions posted in the Chat pod. To activate the Chat pod timestamps select 'Show Timestamps' from the Chat pod options panel icon located in the top right corner of the Chat pod. From that point forward, all new messages will receive a posted time.

Note:
Once timestamps are on in a meeting room, they will stay on for the life of that meeting, even if the meeting is ended and restarted.

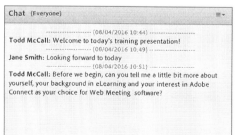

Adobe Connect Chat pod with timestamps.

Chat Pod

Chat Sounds

As a meeting progresses it can be difficult as a presenter to watch the Chat pod actively waiting for messages or questions to appear. To help with this, you can activate 'Chat Sounds' which will make a sound with every message that is submitted to the Chat pod. To turn on chat sounds, select 'Chat Sounds' from the Chat pod options panel icon located in the top right corner of the Chat pod. When selected, a check mark will appear beside this option indicating that is 'on.' This feature will be specific to your meeting experience only, and no other participants will hear your sounds from their computer. Be sure to have your speakers on with a low enough volume so as to not distract the other participants.

Posting Links in Chat Pod

If you want to direct all attendees to a certain website or web page, you can copy - paste, or type the URL into the Chat pod. All URL's typed into the Chat pod become clickable hyper-links automatically.

Adobe Connect Chat pod with hyper-links.

Emailing Chat History

After your meeting is over you may want to export a transcript of all messages or comments submitted to the Chat pod. Perhaps they are questions or comments on your presentation and you want to address these items and modify your presentations for future meetings. To export your chat transcript, select 'Email Chat History' from the Chat pod options panel icon located in the top right corner of the Chat pod.

An email will be sent to the original meeting host with a full detailed transcript of all messages submitted throughout the meeting.

Sample Adobe Connect chat transcript email.

Chat Pod

Clearing Chat

When your meeting is over, you may want to use this meeting room again, but remove all the messages previously submitted. To do so, you will need to clear the chat. By selecting 'Clear Chat' from the Chat pod options panel icon located in the top right corner of the Chat pod, Adobe Connect will remove all the messages submitted to the Chat pod. Note that this will permanently remove all messages so be sure to email a chat transcript first.

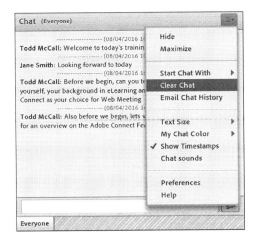

CHAPTER NOTES

CHAPTER NOTES

Sharing Audio (VOIP)

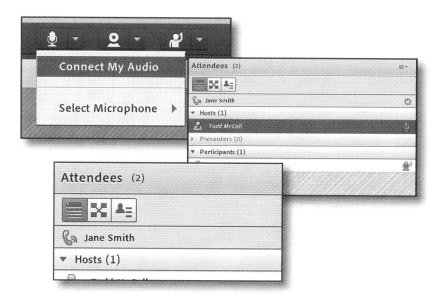

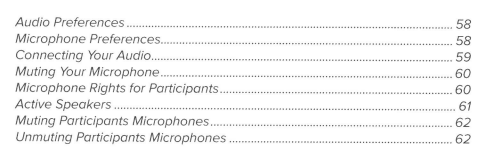

Overview:

Throughout this chapter, we will explore the various audio options available to a host and how Participants can also participate in discussions using a microphone and speaker connected to their computer.

![clock icon]

Time Required:
This chapter should take 45 minutes to explore all the aspects of Adobe Connect VoIP audio sharing.

In This Chapter:

Audio Preferences

Before the start of any Adobe Connect meeting, the Advanced Audio Settings section inside the Microphone section of the preferences menu can be used to customize your audio settings to suit the audience for that specific meeting. To access the Microphone preferences, select 'Preferences' from the Meeting drop down menu. Inside the Preferences panel, select 'Microphone.' Adobe Connect allows you to adjust the Acoustic Echo, Audio quality and Compressed audio quality.

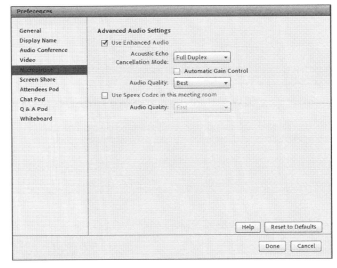

Quick Tip:
if using a separate microphone and speaker set independent from the PC, be sure to use Full Duplex Echo Cancellation to avoid any audio echoing.

Adobe Connect audio preference panel.

Microphone Preferences

When using a microphone, the location of the microphone compared to the speakers could cause an echo. The echo is caused when audio from the meeting is broadcast through your system speakers and picked up by your microphone. By default Echo Cancellation is turned on for all meetings. Please refer to Administrating Adobe Connect – McCall for more information on Echo Cancellation.

Note:
Any audio preference change will saved to that specific meeting room and remain unchanged for every session the meeting room is used for.

Adobe Connect echo preference panel.

Note also that audio being broadcast will use meeting room bandwidth and could lessen the user experience for certain users with slower connection speeds. Adobe Connect allows you to adjust your audio preferences to suit a faster or higher quality audio. Fast audio will result in lower quality sound but will help users with slower connection speeds.

Quick Tip:
If unaware of the connection speed of all Attendees, select 'fast' audio to ensure all Attendees will have no interruption in audio.

Adobe Connect audio quality preference panel.

Connecting Your Audio

To start broadcasting your audio, first connect your audio. To do so, select the drop down icon beside the Microphone icon at the top of your meeting room then select 'Connect My Audio.' This will connect your microphone to your Adobe Connect meeting. If you do not have the Adobe Connect Add-In installed, your Flash player will prompt you to allow access to your computer's microphone.

Adobe Connect audio connection drop down menu.

Note:
Be sure to connect your external microphone before launching your Adobe Connect meeting.

Flash Player Camera and Microphone Access confirmation (when in a meeting without the Adobe Connect Add-In installed).

Muting Your Microphone

Once your microphone is connected it will automatically start broadcasting any audio from your microphone. To stop this broadcast simply click once on the microphone icon at the top of your meeting room window. A white microphone icon indicates your audio is not connected, green indicates that it is connected and broadcasting, and green with a diagonal indicates that your microphone is connected but it is muted.

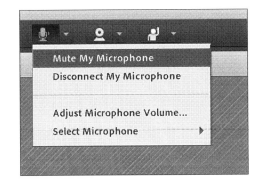

Microphone Rights for Participants

By default, all participants have no access to their microphones, and so they do not have a microphone icon at the top of their meeting room window. To grant microphone rights to participants, mouse-over any participants name in the Attendee panel to access the participant options panel, then select "Enable Microphone,' this will show the microphone icon at the top of that particular attendee's meeting window allowing the attendee to connect their audio.

Note:
Adobe Connect will remember which Attendees were given individual audio rights independently to the Microphone Rights to All Participants option.

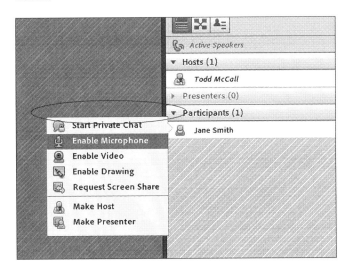

Granting microphone rights individually to attendees can become overwhelming when your attendee list is large. To enable microphone access to all attendees at once, select the drop down icon beside the microphone icon at the top of your meeting room then select 'Microphone Rights For Participants' This will allow all users access to their microphones.

Quick Tip:
The best practice is to enable all microphone rights to all participants prior to starting the meeting.

Active Speakers

During a meeting with many attendees with active microphones, it may be challenging to know who is speaking. Adobe Connect will indicate who is speaking by listing the name of the 'Active Speaker' at the top of the Attendee pod. Additionally Adobe Connect will indicate the 'Active Speaker' by showing small waves beside all attendee's microphone icons in the Attendee pod.

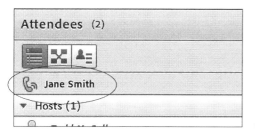

The telephone with waves with show the active speaker.

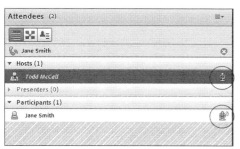

Active speakers with have waves coming from the microphone icon besides their name.

Muting Participants Microphones

From time to time, attendees may have unwanted background noise, or they may have accidentally left their microphone active. As a meeting host, you can simply mute any specific Attendees microphone. To mute an attendee's microphone, mouse-over any participants name in the Attendee pod to access the participant options panel, then select 'Mute Attendee.'

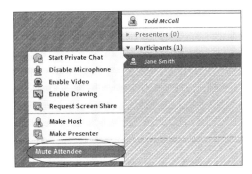

Unmuting Participants Microphones

To unmute an attendee's microphone, mouse-over any participants name in the attendee panel to access the participant Options panel, then select 'Unmute Attendee.' This will turn on and broadcast that attendee's audio.

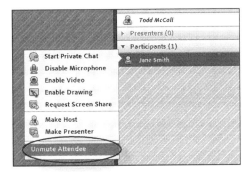

CHAPTER NOTES

Sharing Video

Overview:

Throughout this chapter, we will explore how meeting attendees can share their webcam, how you connect your camera, select different cameras and grant webcam rights to participants.

In This Chapter:

Time Required:
This chapter should take 45 minutes to explore all the aspects of Adobe Connect webcam video sharing.

Sharing Video

Video Preferences

Confirm or change your WebCam preferences before you begin sharing your webcam by selecting 'Preferences' from the Meeting drop down menu, then select the 'Video' tab. There are a few preferences you can adjust for sharing your webcam. Primarily you want to adjust your Video Quality. The slider allows for 4 settings for video Quality, with each setting having a different pixel width and frame rate to help broadcast your video. The lower quality setting is best for the least meeting room bandwidth usage, but it also offers the least detail.

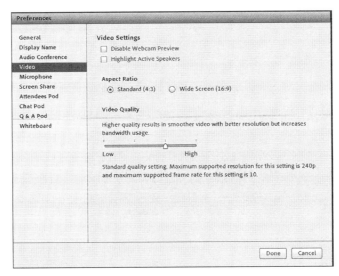

Note:
When you adjust the various Video Quality settings, Adobe connect will indicate the size and frame rate for each setting.

Adobe Connect video preference panel.

Connecting Your Camera

To start sharing video, you must have the Video pod visible (for more information on showing and hiding pods, refer to chapter 11). To start broadcasting your webcam, select the drop down beside the camera icon at the top of your meeting room. By default, only presenters and hosts have webcam rights. Once you select the 'Start My Webcam' option, Adobe Connect will access your default webcam (if set on your system) and a preview will appear in the Video pod.

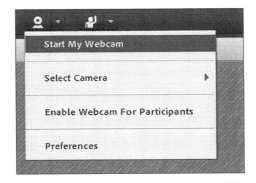

Camera Preview

Adobe Connect will begin by showing you a preview of your camera, this preview is only shown to you and allows you to adjust your camera. Once you are happy with your camera angle and placement, select 'Start Sharing' to begin broadcasting your webcam.

Adobe Connect Video Preview.

Selecting Cameras

If you have multiple cameras connected to your computer, you have the ability to switch between specific cameras. Be sure to connect your camera to your system prior to launching your Adobe Connect meeting room. To select a different camera, select the drop down beside camera icon at the top of your meeting room then select 'Select Camera' where a list of possible cameras will appear. From here you can switch to different cameras. Note that you can only share one camera at a time.

Quick Tip:
Some users when doing webinar will use a ceiling mounted webcam to show the entire meeting including the in-person attendees

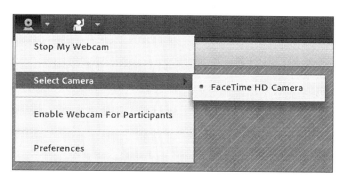

Camera Rights for Participants

By default, only presenters and hosts have access to broadcast their cameras. To allow access to a participant, simply mouse-over the participant in the Attendee pod, then select 'Enable Video.' The participant will now have a camera icon at the top of their meeting and a 'Start My Webcam' button in their Video pod.

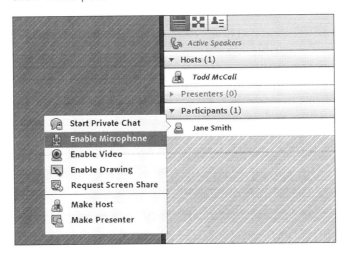

Adobe Connect Attendee options.

If you want to grant video access to all users at once, select the drop down beside camera icon at the top of your meeting room, then select 'Enable Webcam For Participants.' Once this is activated all users will have video rights. Individual camera rights will remain if you choose to deactivate this feature.

Quick Tip:
Auto-Promoting all attendees to presenters will also grant video and microphone rights.

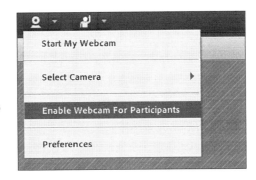

Selecting Camera Layouts

When you have multiple attendees sharing their webcam, you can choose between two different layouts. The first layout shows one camera larger with additional webcam feeds below. The other layout is an equally spaced camera layout where every camera will be equally sized in a grid view. If you are also sharing VOIP Audio, the active speakers camera feed will be highlighted to indicate who is currently speaking.

Single webcam with smaller additional camera 'filmstrip' layout.

Multiple webcam sample 'grid' layout.

Note:
The Adobe Connect Video pod will adjust and re-stack the video feeds based on the number of cameras being shared.

8

Pausing and Stopping Your Webcam Share

At any given time you can pause your camera feed. When you mouse-over your webcam feed in the Video pod, a pause icon will appear where you can pause or resume your video feed. To end your webcam feed, simply select 'Stop' at the top of your Video pod or select the drop down beside camera icon at the top of your meeting room and choose 'Stop My Webcam.'

Note:

When you pause your webcam, all attendees will also be shown a pause icon so they know you have paused your camera. Pausing your webcam is a great way to quickly introduce yourself without continuing to distract yourself or viewers as the presentation progresses.

CHAPTER NOTES

_____

_____

_____

_____

_____

_____

_____

_____

CHAPTER NOTES

Using a Share Pod

Overview:

Throughout this chapter, we will explore how presenters and hosts share a variety of documents as well as brainstorming with the whiteboard and draw overlay.

In This Chapter:

Note:
This chapter should take 45 min to explore all the aspects of the Share pod.

Sharing Documents

The primary function of any web-based meeting is to share and collaborate on documents and presentations. Adobe Connect allows you to upload and share a variety of documents with ease in a Share pod. Share pods allow you to upload PPT, PPTX, SWF and PDF documents, PNG, BMP, GIF and JPG images, as well as FLV, F4V, AVI and MP4 video files.

Adobe Connect Share pod sharing options

To begin sharing a document, open a Share pod (for more information on showing and hiding pods, refer to chapter 11). Before you begin uploading any documents, consider that the size of your document has a direct reflection on upload speed. The larger the document, the longer the upload time so you should upload your documents prior to starting the meeting to avoid any wait time for your attendees. Once a document is shared in Adobe Connect, it is uploaded to the Adobe Connect server and stored in the 'Uploaded Content' folder (further explained in chapter 16).

In the Share pod, select the drop down beside 'Share My Screen' and select 'Share Document.' Adobe Connect will show the 'Select Document to Share' window. From here you will select 'Browse My Computer.'

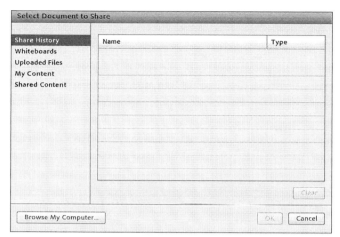

Adobe Connect
document share
loading options.

Quick Tip:
*Every time you load a
document it will be saved to
the Adobe Connect server,
refer to chapter 16 for further
information on managing
uploaded content.*

Sharing PDF Documents

PDF Documents are quick and simple to upload. You can easily post a PDF
for all attendees to view. When posting a PDF, Adobe Connect will convert
each page into a Flash based presentation you can navigate through.

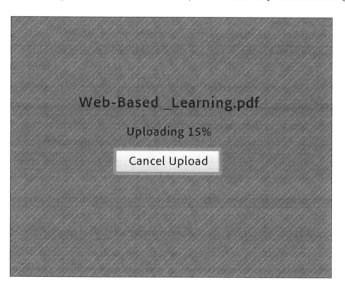

Once your PDF is uploaded, you will notice a page controller similar to
Adobe Acrobat Reader.

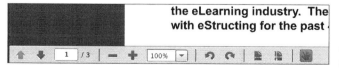

Adobe Connect
PDF controls.

Sharing PowerPoint Presentations

PowerPoint documents are slightly more difficult to load, as animations are converted using a built-in feature called Adobe Presenter which converts your documents for viewing inside Adobe Connect. Because there are more features when sharing a PowerPoint document, more time is required to upload.

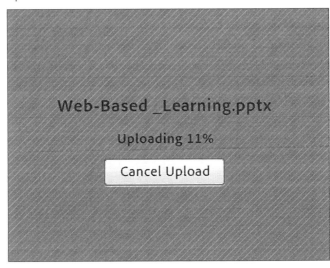

Uploading prompt.

Note:
If your presentation has web-links or videos, they will not be shared. In this situation, it would be best to share your screen, then use PowerPoint to share your presentation.

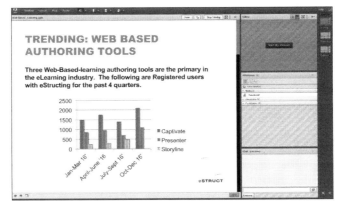

PowerPoint presentation loaded into Adobe Connect.

Annotating a Presentation

Once your document is loaded, you can easily annotate a document with the 'Draw' feature. This essentially pauses your document and allows a whiteboard overlay. To annotate, select 'Draw' at the top of your Share pod and the drawing features will show on the left side of your document. You can draw with a marker, highlight, type or create shapes over top of your document.

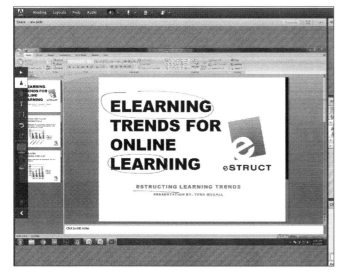

Annotated presentation.

Note:
By default, only hosts and presenters can draw on a presentation. Hover your mouse over any participant in the Attendee pod and select 'Enable Draw' to grant drawing rights to any participant.

Quick Tip:
When annotating over a presentation, you can export your drawing by selecting 'Export Snapshot' from the Share pod options.

Navigating Through a Document

All multi-page documents shared inside the Share pod will have a navigation menu at the bottom of the Share pod. With a PowerPoint document, you will have access to a 'Table of Contents' panel which will also show any slide notes that were created in the original document. By selecting the Back /Forth icons you can change the page that is displayed to all the meeting Attendees. All presenters and meeting hosts have access to the page navigation panel.

Adobe Connect presentation controls.

9

Synch On – only Presenter
Navigates
Synch Off – hSUS Nov

Synchronizing Your Document with Your Audience

By default, multi-page documents are controlled by the host or presenter. Whichever page the host or presenter displays will be synchronized to all attendees. You can choose to desynchronize the document by selecting the 'Sync' button at the bottom of the Share pod. This allows all users to navigate through the document individually. When you re-select the 'Sync' button, all attendees will have their document put back to the page of the presenter or host who re-selected the 'Sync' button.

Quick Tip:
The 'Sync' button is a great tool if you have attendees connecting from remote locations or with poor internet connections, this allows them to navigate themselves without experiencing any delays.

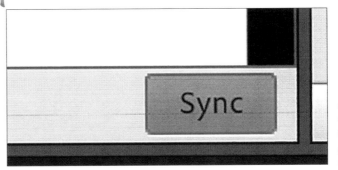

Adobe Connect synchronization button found with all multi-page presentations and documents.

Sharing Images

Images are shared just like all other documents, in that you have the ability to annotate on any image. The only difference is a single image will not have any navigation controls.

Note:
All images shared in the Share pod also have the option to 'Draw,' adding a whiteboard overlay on top of the image.

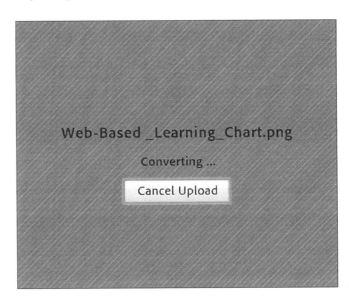

Web-Based _Learning_Chart.png

Converting ...

Cancel Upload

Uploading prompt.

Sharing Videos

Adobe Connect will allow you to share video files. Similar to larger documents, more time is required to upload based on the length of your video. It is strongly recommended to pre-upload a video prior to starting your meeting to prevent wasting time waiting for files to upload.

MP4 Video loaded into Adobe Connect.

Sharing a Whiteboard

You can collaborate on ideas, draw a workflow or brainstorm ideas easily inside Adobe Connect using the whiteboard feature. To share a whiteboard, select the drop down beside 'Share My Screen' inside any Share pod and select 'Share Whiteboard'. The drawing tools provided are the same tools found when annotating a document. By default only hosts and presenters have drawing rights. To enable drawing, mouse-over any participant in the Attendee pod and select 'Enable Drawing.' Alternatively, you can select 'Enable Participants to draw' in the main Whiteboard pod options.

Note:
Each whiteboard can have unlimited layers, by clicking on the right arrow at the bottom left of the Whiteboard Share pod.

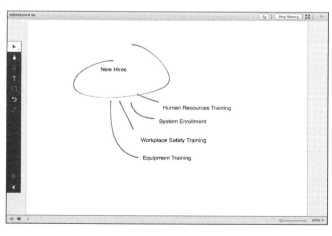

Brainstorming and collaboration with the Adobe Connect whiteboard.

Sharing Previously Shared Content

Once you have uploaded a document for sharing, Adobe Connect will store that document in the 'Uploaded Content' folder on the Adobe Connect server. You can recall any document previously uploaded quickly and easily without having to upload it again. In the Share pod, select the drop down beside 'Share My Screen' and immediately Adobe Connect will show all the 'Share History' for your meeting. You can select any of the documents to reload them. This is highly recommended for all meetings, allowing the meeting host to pre-load a document, stop sharing it and have it waiting in the share history to be easily shared again.

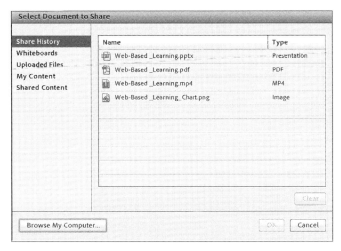

Adobe Connect share upload prompt.

Note:
By selecting any document in the share history, you can delete it from the folder by selecting 'Clear.'

CHAPTER NOTES

CHAPTER NOTES

Note, File Share & Web Link Pods

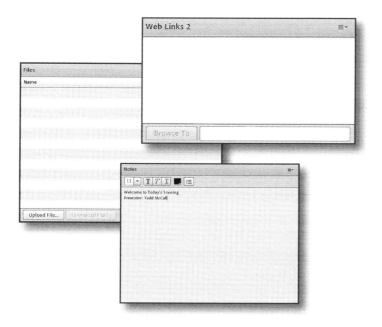

Overview:

Throughout this chapter, we will explore how to access the Note, Web Link and File Share pods. These pods will be used throughout various meetings to list information, distribute in-meeting documentation and link attendees to helpful online resources.

In This Chapter:

Note:
This chapter should take 30 minutes to explore all the aspects of the Note, File and Web Link pods.

Note Pods

Throughout a meeting you may want to post brief notes as a helpful tip to your attendees. These Note pods can include conference call numbers, meeting start times or even meeting agendas. Most often the Note pod is used during a webinar when the Chat pod is not visible. This allows the webinar to go un-interrupted still show a meeting agenda indicating when a Q&A will happen. To show the Note pod select Notes from the Pods drop down menu.

Adobe Connect
Note pod.

Quick Tip:
Often presenters use the Note pod as a welcome note describing the days lesson before a meeting begins.

Setting Colors and Fonts

To identify critical information, or draw attention to specific information in the Note pod, any meeting host or presenter can modify the text in the Note pod. Type can be modified in a variety of typical fashions including the font size, adding emphasis such as Bold, Italic, and Underline. In addition, you can change the color of every character individually as well as create a bulleted list.

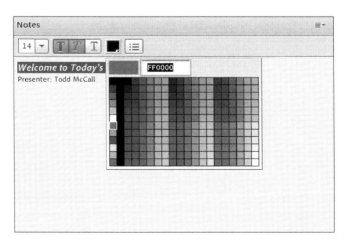

Adobe Connect Note
pod text color options.

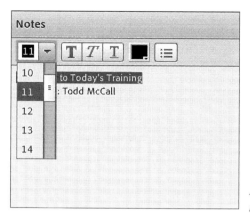

Quick Tip:
To control the flow of a meeting, presenters and hosts often hide the Chat pod so as to not distract the audience, and show a Note pod explaining the meeting agenda.

Adobe Connect Note pod font size options.

File Share Pod

Before your meeting begins you may want attendees to download various files to help guide them through your presentation or webinar. The File Share pod makes this very easy as you can upload and share any file. Additionally the File Share pod can create a list of files that can be renamed individually. To show the File Share pod select File Share from the Pods drop down menu.

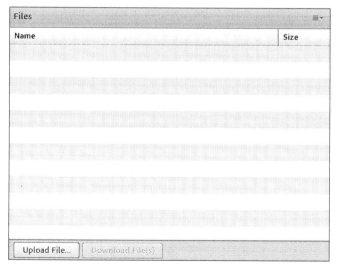

Adobe Connect File Share pod.

Adding Files

Once the File Share pod is visible, select the 'Upload File' from the File Share pod options or select the 'Upload File' button in the bottom left corner. Adobe Connect will then prompt you to select a file from previously uploaded documents. This makes the File Share pod very quick as it will list all files already uploaded to the Adobe Connect server. Files can also be uploaded directly from your system by selecting 'Browse computer.'

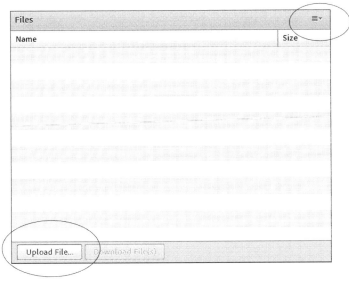

Note:
You can have more than one File Share pod; one for every presentation or course taught, this will help you prepare your meeting room for multiple use.

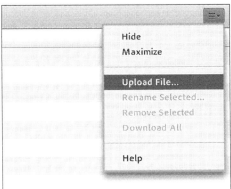

Uploading files directly from your computer to the File Share pod.

Removing / Renaming Files

After a file has been uploaded and listed in the File Share pod it can be easily renamed to help identify the file. For example a file 'March_Quarterly_Report_Final_Version.PDF' can be easily changed to 'March Meeting Report.' To rename a file, select the file in the File Share pod list then select 'Rename Selected...' from the File Share pod options. Adobe Connect will then allow you to rename the file. If a file needs to be replaced, the first step is to remove the current file in the File Share pod. To delete a file, select the file in the File Share pod list then select 'Delete File' from the File Share pod options.

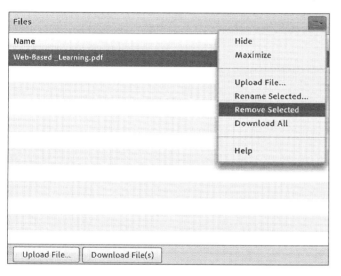

Note:
Always be sure to upload your files in advance to save any uploading time.

Web Link Pod

During a meeting, Hosts and Presenters may want to send attendees to a specific Web URL's for reference material. Hosts and presenters can either post these links or 'Push' all attendees to this URL. To show the Web Link pod select Web Link from the Pods drop down menu.

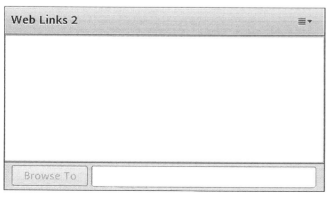

Adobe Connect Web Link pod.

Adding Links

To add a link into the Web Link pod, select 'Add Link' from the Web Link pod options icon in the top right corner of the Web Link pod.

Adobe Connect will prompt you to add a URL Name and URL Path. The URL Path would be where you type or copy/paste the URL from your browser that you want to share. The URL name would be any text you like to describe or label the link.

Note:
Similar to the File Share pod, you can have more than one Web Link pod, one for every presentation or course taught. This will help you prepare your meeting room for multiple use.

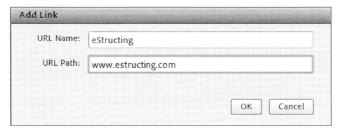

Add Link dialog box.

For Example:
URL Name: eStructing Workbooks Website
URL Path: http://www.estructing.com
Be careful not to confuse these two when adding a link

Removing Links

After a meeting has finished it may be important to remove the posted links for a different course or a different set of attendees. To remove a link, select the link in the Web Link pod, then select 'Remove Selected' from the Web Link pod options. This will remove the link permanently from the list.

Quick Tip:
Forcing all attendees to a website could result in a loss of attendee engagement as they will be redirected to another URL and away from the meeting room.

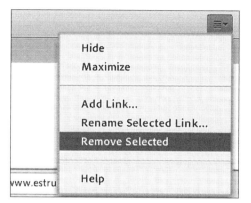

Forcing Participants to Links

After a link has been posted in the Web Link pod, all users can select that link and hit 'Browse to' and they will be directed to that URL individually. If a host or presenter does the same process, all participants will be forced to that URL. Note that when a host or presenter selects this, they will be redirecting their attendees away from the Adobe Connect meeting.

CHAPTER NOTES

_____

_____

_____

_____

_____

_____

_____

_____

_____

_____

Customizing Pods

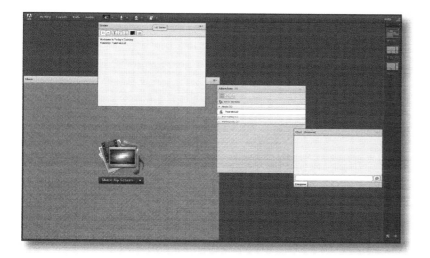

Overview:

Throughout this chapter, we will explore how to customize a meeting room by changing the size of pods as well as changing the layout of the screen back to the default.

In This Chapter:

Note:
This chapter should take 45 minutes to explore all the aspects of customizing the Adobe Connect pods.

Setting Pod Names

To help organize your visible pods, you can rename the pods individually. By default, pods are pre-named, for example Share 1, Share 2 etc. To rename a pod, double-click on the pod's name. The pod name will highlight allowing you to rename it.

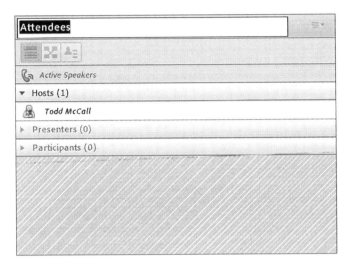

Rename any pod by double clicking the title of any pod.

Once you have renamed your pod, simply hit the Return / Enter key to save the name.

Quick Tip:
Naming pods is a great way to keep your meeting organized.

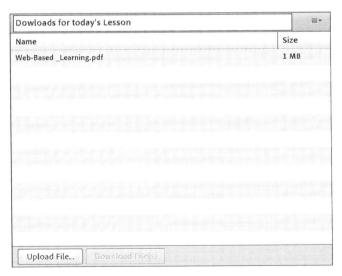

Pods can accept any custom name.

Hiding Pods

All pods can be easily hidden and shown at any time. To hide a pod, select 'Hide' from the pod options. The pod will disappear from the meeting room but will not be deleted.

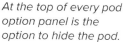

Quick Tip:
To save time during a meeting, have a presentation loaded and ready for sharing. To do this, show a new Share pod, load a presentation, rename the Share pod, then hide it.

At the top of every pod option panel is the option to hide the pod.

Re-Opening Pods

To reshow a pod, select the Pods drop down menu and then scroll down to the pod you want to show. You can have multiple versions of every pod except the Attendee, Video and Q&A Pods. It is not uncommon to have multiple Share pods.

Note:
You can have as many pods as you like on the screen but the more pods you show, the more difficult the content will be to read.

Customizing Pods

Managing Pods

As your meeting room gets reused or becomes more complex with multiple presentations and Note pods, you will need to start organizing and removing unwanted pods. To delete pods, including hidden pods, select the Pods drop down menu then select 'Manage Pods.' Adobe Connect will open a 'Manage Pods' dialog box listing all pods in your meeting including hidden pods.

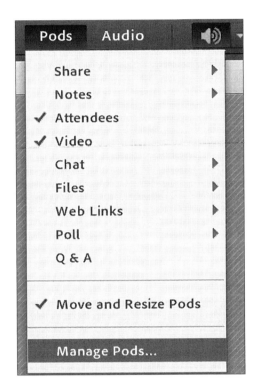

Note:
Before your start a new session of any meeting room, be sure to check the unused pods and delete any unnecessary pods.

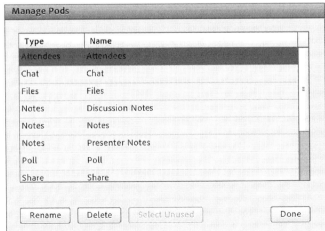

The Adobe Connect Manage Pod panel allows you to find, rename or delete every existing pod in a meeting room.

Deleting Pods and Unused Pods

Hidden pods are also referred to as 'Unused' pods. After you have shown a presentation, or after you show a Note pod, you may hide it and no longer need it. To delete one or more pods that are not needed, hit the 'Select Unused' button, this will highlight all pods currently hidden in your meeting room, then hit 'Delete.' You can also rename a pod here by selecting the pod in the Manage Pod list and selecting 'Rename.'

Quick Tip:
Additional pods do not slow down your meeting, but by deleting unused pods you help keep your meeting room organized.

Moving Pods

All pods can be moved to create a custom meeting experience. You can have many pods visible on the screen at one time without affecting the speed of your meeting room. To move a pod, simply click and hold the title or top of the pod and drag it to a new position. Every pod in Adobe Connect is modular and can be moved anywhere in the meeting. To ensure a pod can be moved, select the Pods drop down menu, then make sure 'Move and Resize Pods' has a check mark beside it.

Note:
If you attempt to move a pod, and it will not move, be sure to check that 'Move and Resize Pods' is selected in the Pods drop down menu.

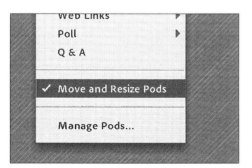

Customizing Pods

Resizing Pods

To resize a pod, move your cursor to the top right corner until a double ended arrow appears then, click, hold and drag the top corner to resize the pod. As the pod resizes, so does the content inside the pod.

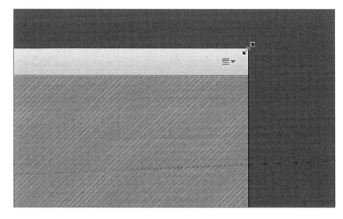

Notice the double-ended arrow that appears when you move your cursor over the edge of a pod.

Note:
Only Hosts can resize pods.

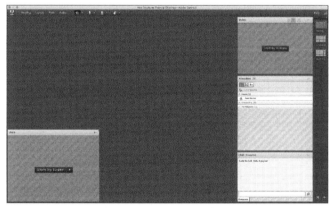

By click, hold and dragging on the edge or corner of a pod you can resize it to fit any dimension in your meeting room.

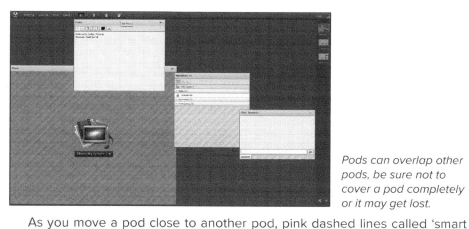

Quick Tip:
When you show a new pod, it will automatically fill the available space in the meeting room.

Pods can overlap other pods, be sure not to cover a pod completely or it may get lost.

As you move a pod close to another pod, pink dashed lines called 'smart guides' will appear allowing you to align two pods together. You can also uses these guides to evenly space pods.

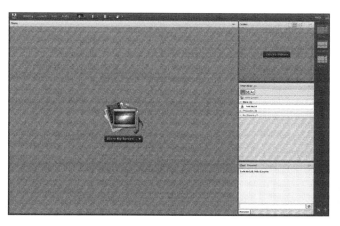

The pink dashed smart guides appear to help keep your pods aligned and spaced equally.

Maximizing Pods

Once a meeting is running, some presenters prefer to remove any distracting pods inside a meeting. For example, a presenter may choose to remove the Chat or Attendee pod to draw attention to a presentation in the Share pod. A faster way to emphasize a certain pod is to 'Maximize' the pod. This will expand the size of the pod to occupy the entire meeting area. This will be done for all attendee's screens and cover up any other pods in the meeting room. To maximize a pod, select 'Maximize' from the pod options in the top right corner of the pod.

Almost every pod can be maximized to occupy the entire meeting space.

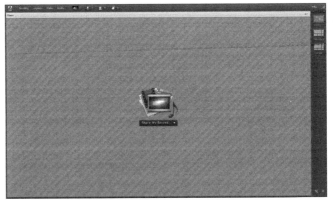

Note:
You can move a pod on top of any other pod. However, this can be a problem as pods get lost, be sure to not overlap pods completely.

Restoring a Pod

When a pod is maximized it will cover up all other visible pods, this is only temporary and can be easily restored back to its original size. To restore a pod, select 'Restore' from the pod options in the top right corner of the pod.

To return to the previous size of a pod, select restore from the pod options.

Full Screen View

   Toggle

To help the viewing experience for all users, every Share pod has the ability to show in 'Full Screen.' Full screen mode will maximize the Share Pod, remove the title bar and occupy the entire meeting window. This experience is independent to every user. To maximize a Share pod with a document, select the four arrow icon in the top right corner of the Share pod.

Quick Tip:
All users can view a document in Full Screen independently to maximize a document, this is helpful for users with smaller screens.

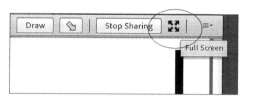

The four arrow icon will make the Share Pod visible as Full Screen when selected.

Additionally you can access Full Screen by selecting the Share pod drop down menu in the top right corner of the Share pod, then select 'Full Screen.'

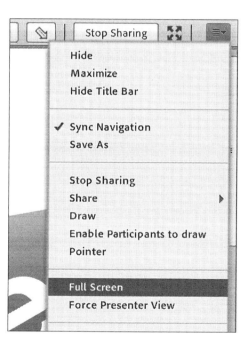

Forcing Presenter View

Since a full screen mode is independent to each user's experience and not to all of the attendees, Adobe Connect can force the presenter's view and make all attendees have the same experience as the presenter with a feature called "Force Presenter View.' To enable this, select 'Force Presenter View' from the Share pod option. This will make the Share pod expand to full screen for all users. To end this, you will need to turn off full screen mode then deselect 'Force Presenter View.'

Quick Tip:
When you turn on Force Presenter View, all users will have the same viewing experience as the presenter or host, be sure to tell your attendees how to restore or exit full screen mode if you turn off Force Presenter View.

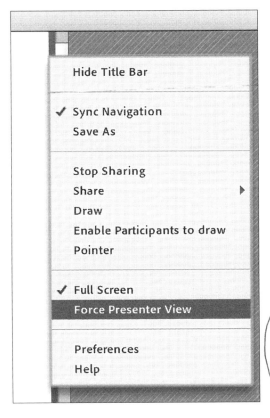

When you turn on Force Presenter View and then go full screen with a pod, this will force the full screen view for all Attendees.

Resetting Layouts

As your meeting progresses, you may end up with many unorganized pods in various places. The easiest way to re-organize all your pods is to reset the meeting room layouts.

Quick Tip:
When planning to reuse a meeting room, you should reset the layout.

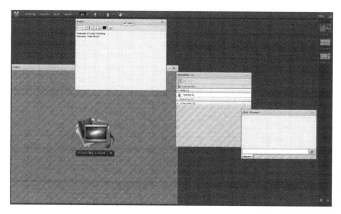

It is easy for a meeting room to become unorganized.

To resent layouts, select 'Reset Layouts' from the Layouts drop down menu.

Layouts	Pods	Auc

Create New Layout...

• Sharing

Discussion

Collaboration

Manage Layouts...

Reset Layouts

Close Layout Bar

When you reset your layouts, Adobe Connect will warn you that when you reset layouts, all pods will be resized, some pods will be hidden to take the meeting room back to the default template layout.

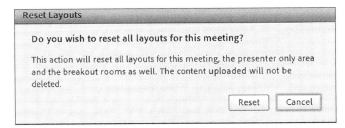

Resetting layouts will hide some pods, but not delete them.

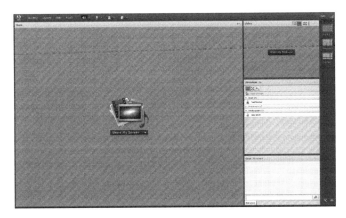

Resetting your layout will return your layout to the original default layout set when the meeting was created.

CHAPTER NOTES

CHAPTER NOTES

12

Overview:

Throughout this chapter, we will explore how meeting hosts and presenters can share their screen and select specific screens, applications or windows. We will also explore how to grant screen sharing permissions to participants and request control of other participants' computers.

In This Chapter:

Note:
This chapter should take 60 minutes to explore all the aspects of the sharing a screen.

Screen Sharing Basics

Adobe Connect will not let you share some specific document types including Photoshop, Microsoft Excel or Word Documents directly in a Share pod. To share any document in their native application, Adobe Connect allows presenters and hosts to 'Share My Screen.' This option will broadcast a live feed of your computer.

Share Quality Preferences

When sharing your screen, Adobe Connect can share the feed in four different resolutions to help keep bandwidth down. If your audience is experiencing any lag during a screen share, the host can easily adjust the quality without interrupting the meeting.

Note:
When the connection speed of your entire audience is unknown, use the Medium or Low quality setting to ensure a good meeting experience for your audience.

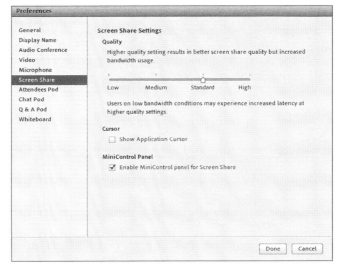

Adobe Connect screen share preference panel.

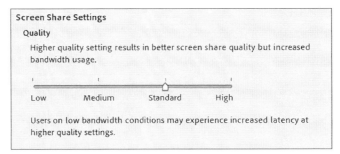

Different share qualities use different screen refresh rates and pixel dimensions, for faster screen refresh, select 'Low.'

Cursors

Before you begin sharing a screen be sure to turn on the 'Show Application Cursor' if you are demonstrating software or a specific application, this way all attendees will be able to see what and where you are selecting when you are sharing your screen.

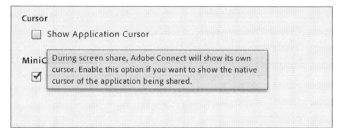

Share Screen

To begin sharing a screen, you must have a Share pod visible. From the Share pod, select 'Share My Screen' or select 'Share' - 'My Screen' from the Share pod options.

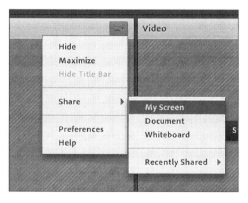

Screen sharing can be turned on from the Share Pod option panel or by selecting 'Share My Screen' in the center of a Share pod.

Note:
By default only hosts and presenters can share their screen.

Connect Add-In

Screen sharing is one of the few functions that require the Adobe Connect Add-In to be installed. When a presenter who does not have the Add-In installed attempts to share their screen, they will be asked to install it. This process is quick and easy and during the process, Adobe Connect will automatically remove that user, close their Adobe Connect meeting room window, and re-enter them into the meeting via the Adobe Connect Add-In.

Note:
For more information on installing the Adobe Connect Add-In, refer to page XIV.

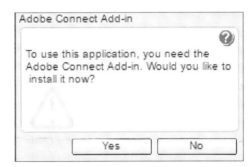

Installing the Adobe Connect Add-In is very quick and simple to install.

The Adobe Connect Add-In is separate software and the meeting will be launched with this application. The next time an Adobe Connect user connects to a meeting URL in their internet browser, Adobe Connect will check to see if the Add-In is installed and launch a meeting with the Add-In. Users do not need to launch the Add-In in order to connect to a meeting.

Quick Tip:
The Adobe Connect Add-In installer will require the user to have administrator rights to their system.

After the Adobe Connect Add-In is installed, all meetings will appear in a separate window from the internet browser.

Once an attendee selects 'Share My Screen,' Adobe Connect will ask which part of the screen the attendee wants to share. The host or presenter will then be asked if they want to share their whole desktop, an application, or a specific window.

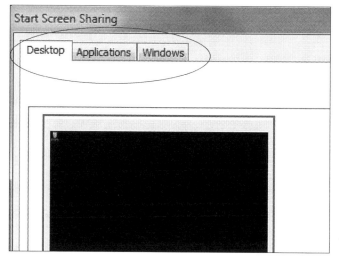

Adobe Connect Screen Share options.

Sharing Desktop

Adobe Connect Screen sharing allows you to share your desktop entirely. If two monitors are in use, Adobe Connect will allow you to select the monitor to share. Be aware that your desktop will be show in its entirety including email notifications etc.

Quick Tip:
Turn off all notifications when sharing a desktop to avoid unwanted message or reminders from popping up on the screen during a presentation.

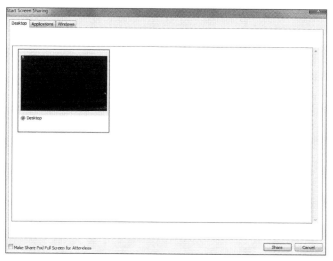

When sharing your desktop, Adobe Connect will ask which desktop to share in the event of multiple desktops.

12

Sharing Applications

Adobe Connect screen sharing allows you to select a specific application to share, all other applications will not be visible. Additional notifications from other software, the start menu etc., will not be shown.

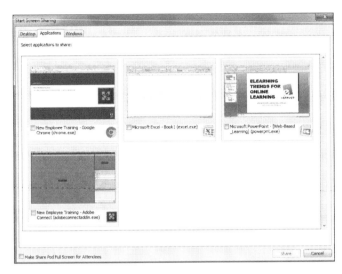

When sharing an application, Adobe Connect shows a preview of all open applications to be shared.

Quick Tip:
By sharing an application only, Adobe Connect will not show any notifications from other applications.

Sharing Windows

Adobe Connect screen sharing allows you to select a specific application window to share, if there are additional windows of that specific software, they will not be shown. For example, if 5 different Excel documents are open, only the one selected will be visible to the meeting attendees.

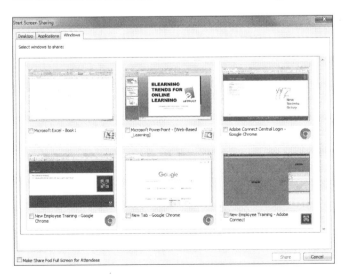

When sharing a window, Adobe Connect shows a preview of all open windows that can be shared.

The Mini Controller

Once screen sharing has started, Adobe Connect will disappear allowing you begin sharing a presentation or software. Adobe connect will show a 'Mini Controller' which is not shown to the attendees. From here you can access almost all of the meeting room pod features.

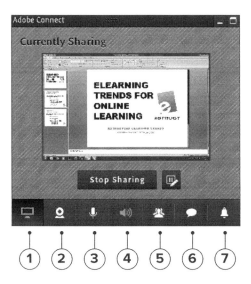

1   **Preview Screen**
2   **Camera Controls**
3:   **Microphone On/Off Control**
4:   **Speaker Volume**
5:   **Attendee Pod**
6:   **Chat Pod**
7:   **Notifications**

Pausing and Annotating

By selecting the Pause button in the share preview section of the mini controller, the Adobe Connect meeting window will reopen and show a paused screen capture of your shared desktop/application/window. This screen caption will have a whiteboard overlay allowing Attendees to annotate the screen capture.

Note:
The mini controller can be moved anywhere or minimized if interfering with a presenters navigation. This menu is not displayed to your audience.

Pause and Annotate button in the preview section of the Adobe Connect mini controller.

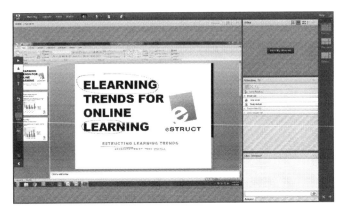

Paused and annotated screen share of a Microsoft Powerpoint presentation.

To resume a screen share, select the 'Resume' button at the top of the paused screen share inside the Share pod.

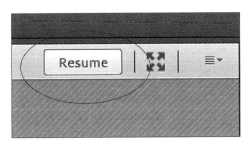

Resume button found in the top right of the share pod allows you to stop annotating and resume the shared screen.

Note:
Only attendees with drawing rights can annotate a paused screen share.

Ending a Screen Share

To end a screen share, select the 'Stop Sharing' button inside the preview screen section of the mini controller.

Requesting a Screen Share

Often a presenter will ask to see a Participants screen. To do so, mouse over their name in the Attendee pod, and select 'Request Screen Share.'

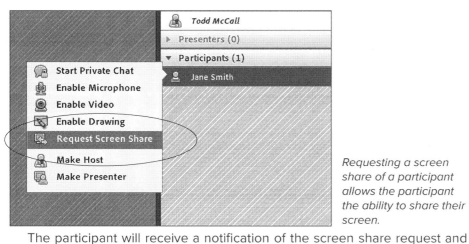

Requesting a screen share of a participant allows the participant the ability to share their screen.

The participant will receive a notification of the screen share request and decide to accept of decline the request.

Participants will receive a request to start a screen share.

Requesting Control

As an attendee shares their screen, another host or presenter can request control of the attendee's machine. To request control, select the 'Request Control' button at the top of the screen sharing window.

A host or presenter can request control of a screen share anytime doing the share.

Once a different attendee has requested control of a screen share, the first attendee (the one already sharing their screen) will receive a control request in the notification section of the mini controller.

CHAPTER NOTES

CHAPTER NOTES

Meeting Polls

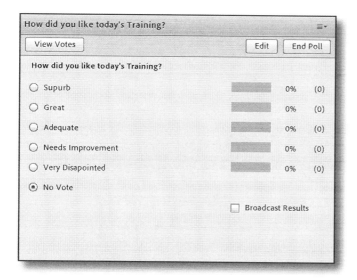

Overview:

Throughout this chapter, we will explore how to create, run, edit, and broadcast the results of Multiple Choice, Multiple Answer and Short Answer Polls.

Note:
This chapter should take 45 minutes to explore all the aspects of the Poll pod.

In This Chapter:

Creating a Multiple Choice Poll

Throughout a meeting, presenters and hosts can run polls to collect data. To create a poll, select 'Poll' from the Pods drop down menu, then select 'Add New Poll.' Adobe Connect will add a Poll pod to the meeting room and the default question type will be Multiple Choice. Now, add the 'Question,' then list the possible answers on separate lines below one another.

Note:
Poll pods automatically get renamed with the question being asked in the poll.

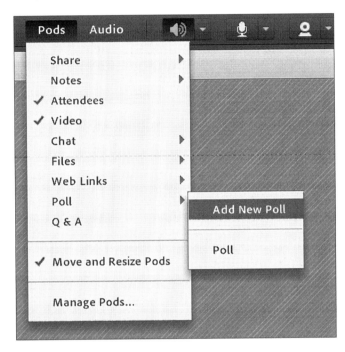

Adobe Connect will allow as many Poll pods as you need.

Blank Poll pods are always Multiple Choice by default.

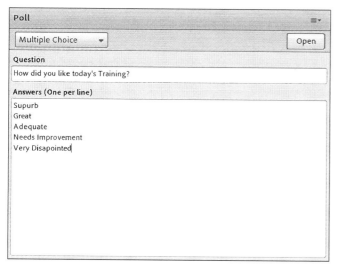

Multiple Answer Poll pod ready to be opened.

Creating a Multiple Answer Poll

If your poll question could have multiple answers, change the question type from Multiple Choice to Multiple Answers.

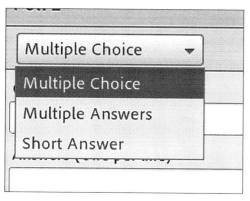

The question type drop down menu allows you to change to a Multiple Answer or Short Answer question.

Creating a Short Answer Poll

If the Poll pod is intended to receive custom answers such as feedback, the question type can be changed to a Short Answer where attendees can type their response.

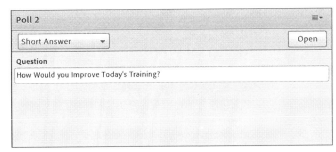

Short Answer poll ready to be opened.

Opening a Poll

Once the Poll pod question is ready for responses, the host or presenter can select 'Open.' Once a poll is open, it will remain open until the poll is ended. To open a poll, select the 'Open' button at the top right corner of a Poll pod.

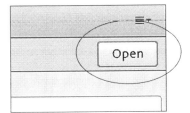

Note:
Every time a poll is opened and closed, the data will be stored with the session number in which the poll was run.

Presenter View

Presenters and hosts will see the poll results as they are entered and all attendees can submit an answer to the poll including meeting hosts.

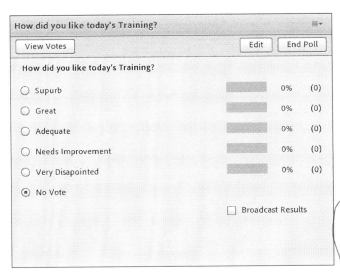

Presenters and hosts receive a different view of an open poll than the participants.

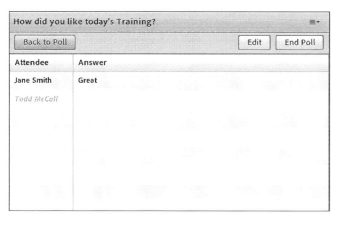

Quick Tip:
Broadcasting the results can often skew the responses as attendees will submit answers based on trending responses.

Open Poll Pod with responses.

Participant View

Participants will only see the possible answers they can choose from, unless the presenter selects 'Broadcast Results.' This option can help all attendees see the general responses that all attendees are submitting.

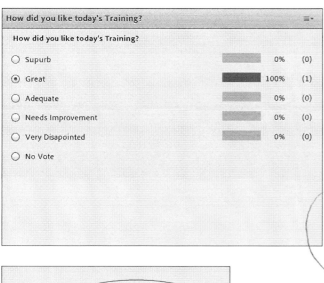

Participant view of a poll pod with the results being broadcasted.

Ending a Poll

When all the attendees have responded to a poll, or when the presenter is ready to move on, the meeting host or presenter will close the poll by selecting the 'End Poll' button. This will store the poll data on the Adobe Connect server.

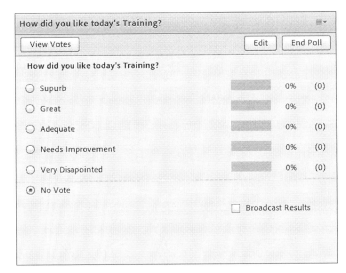

Once a poll has been ended, the Host can hide the Poll pod, it will not be deleted and can be reused again.

Note:
Ending a poll will store the data on the Adobe Connect server.

Editing a Poll

To reuse a poll question, but change the question type after a poll has been run, select the 'Edit' button. From here the host or presenter can edit the question or the question type.

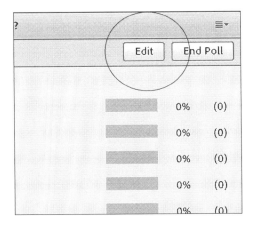

Polls can be easily edited at any time during a meeting.

Viewing Votes

When the presenter or host selects 'View Votes,' all of the participants answers will be listed.

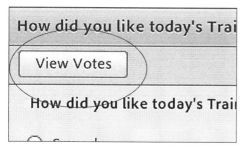

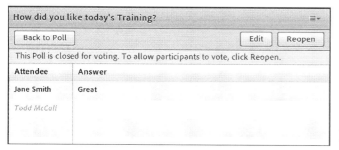

Presenter view of all votes from a poll.

Poll Results

After a poll has been closed, or the meeting has ended, all poll data will be saved to the Adobe Connect Server. To access this data, select 'Manage Meeting Information' from the Meeting drop down menu to access the Adobe Connect Central meeting information.

Note:
Poll results will be available immediately on the Adobe Connect Central Meeting Information page.

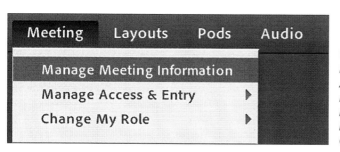

When 'Manage Meeting Information' Is selected, Adobe Connect will navigate to the Meeting Information page inside Adobe Connect Central.

Meeting Polls

Once inside the Adobe Connect Central meeting information, select the 'Report' submenu to access meeting room usage data.

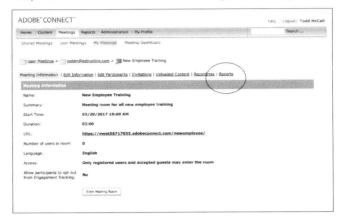

Adobe Connect Central meeting information page.

Select the 'By Question' submenu to access the poll results. The report submenu will show all the polls that have been opened and closed during the meeting.

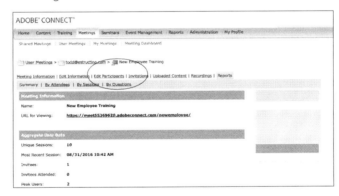

Adobe Connect Central meeting usage report page will contain the poll data.

Select 'view user responses' to see a full report of all submitted answers.

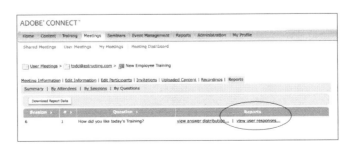

Poll data can be displayed by answer distribution and individual user responses.

To save all of this data to your system, select 'Download Report Data' to download a .CSV file containing the report data.

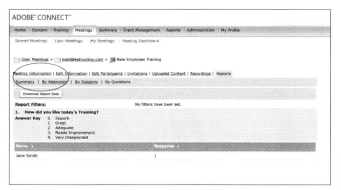

Poll data can be downloaded per session.

CHAPTER NOTES

_____

_____

_____

_____

_____

_____

_____

_____

_____

_____

_____

_____

_____

_____

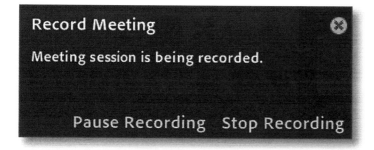

Recording a Meeting

Overview:

Throughout this chapter, we will explore how meeting hosts can record their meetings. Additionally we will fully explore how to find, make public, share and export meeting recordings.

Note:
This chapter should take 30 minutes to explore all the aspects of recording a meeting.

In This Chapter:

Starting a Meeting Recording

All meeting hosts have the ability to record a meeting. All VoIP audio, screen sharing and messages will be recorded from a Participant's view. To start recording a meeting, select 'Record Meeting....' from the Meeting drop down menu.

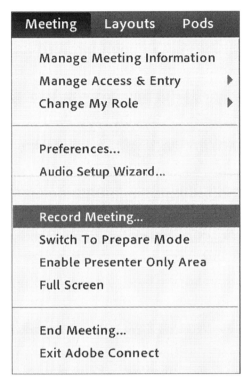

Note:
If using a conference call, the audio will not be recorded unless you have previously integrated your teleconferencing line with the meeting room.

Quick Tip:
Meeting recordings will be automatically named if you do not change the name. Recording Name and Summary can be changed in the Adobe Connect Central at any time after the recording has ended.

Adobe Connect will prompt you to name your recording.

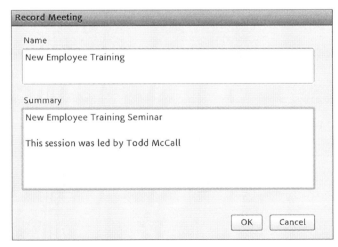

Adobe Connect recording naming window.

Pausing Your Recording

Once the recording has started, a red dot will appear in the top right corner of your meeting, and is visible to the host only. When selecting this dot, Adobe Connect will show you the recording options, including pausing.

Live meetings may include breaks, this would make for a long recording. To avoid this, select 'Pause Recording' to temporarily stop the recording, this will not show when reviewing the recording.

Quick Tip:
You can start / stop your meeting recording as many times as you want, each recording will be saved as a unique recoding.

Adobe Connect recording menu can be accessed by the meeting host by selecting the red record icon in the top right of the meeting once a recording has started.

Ending Your Recording

Once the meeting is over you can easily stop the recording. To stop the recording select the red recording icon in the top right corner of the meeting room then select 'Stop Recording.' Once a meeting recording has stopped, it cannot be restarted. You can start a new recording but it will be a separate file from the previous recording.

Note:
Private chatting, including host / attendee private chatting will not be recorded.

Locating Your Recordings

After each recording session Adobe Connect will make an individual recording file found in Adobe Connect Central. To locate these recordings select 'Manage Meeting Information' from the Meeting drop down menu. Adobe Connect will navigate to Adobe Connect Central and from there, select the 'Recordings' tab for the meeting.

Note:
The URL of a recording cannot be customized.

From the 'Recordings' Tab, Adobe Connect will list all recordings from your meeting. Each file can be made public, edited and downloaded as an MP4 or FLV file.

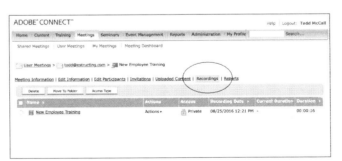

Making your Recordings Public

If a meeting needs to be made public and shared with other participants, it can be unlocked and made available publicly to anyone with the recording URL. To make a recording public, select the check box beside the recording you want to make public, then select the 'Access Type' button.

Quick Tip:
Meeting recordings do not use much space but over time can add up. To make sure you are not approaching maximum capacity, use the Administration tab inside the Adobe Connect Central and check disk usage.

Adobe Connect will give you the option to make the meeting 'Private' or 'Public.'

Adding a Password

Once you select 'Public,' Adobe Connect will allow you to set a password to access the meeting. Once finished, select the 'Save' button. Public meeting recordings do not have to have a password but this will help if confidential material is shared during the meeting.

Note:
Public recordings can be shared to anyone who has the URL and password if added.

Recording a Meeting

Sharing The Recording

After a meeting recording has been made public, it can be easily shared. To share your meeting recording, highlight the meeting recording URL, and copy/paste this recording URL into an email.

Taking Your Recordings Offline

Meeting recordings can be downloaded for use outside Adobe Connect. The recording can be downloaded as either an MP4 or FLV video file and with different resolution settings. To make a meeting recording available offline, select the check box beside the recording, then select 'Make Offline' from the actions drop down menu.

Note:
Meeting recording URL's cannot be shared with email invitations directly from Adobe Connect, then only way to share is to manually copy / paste the URL in a separate email.

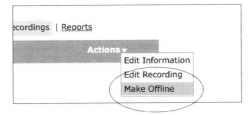

Adobe Connect will prompt you to adjust your screen resolution and expand the meeting window to best match the original meeting.

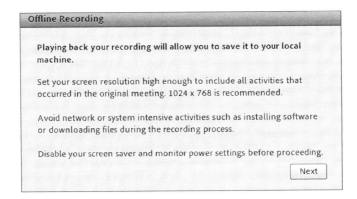

Adobe Connect will then prompt you to select the type of meeting file and the resolution you want to be generated before exporting your file. Once you select 'Proceed with Offline Recording' Adobe Connect will launch the meeting recording and start the file generation.

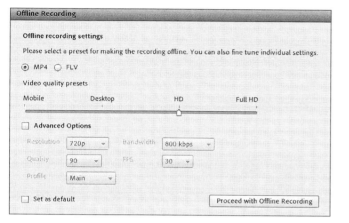

Quick Tip:
Generating a meeting recording in MP4 or FLV formats require the meeting recording to play in it's entirety to generate the offline file. For example, if a meeting was 2 hours in length, it will take 2 hours to generate the MP4 or FLV file.

CHAPTER NOTES

_____

_____

_____

_____

_____

_____

_____

_____

_____

_____

_____

_____

_____

_____

Ending a Meeting

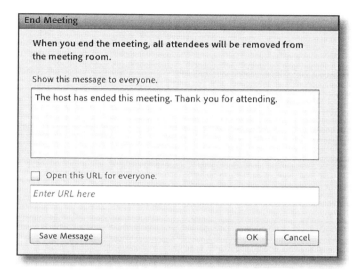

Overview:

Throughout this chapter, we will explore how to end a meeting, setting an ending message, forcing users to a specific website and resetting your meeting room for future sessions.

Note:
This chapter should take 15 minutes to explore all the aspects of ending a meeting.

In This Chapter:

Ending the Meeting

When a meeting has come to its ending, the meeting room will stay active as long as the meeting host is present. When the meeting is 'Ended,' attendees will no longer see any of the active pods and receive a message screen that can be customized with a message to attendees. In addition, if you want to send the attendees to a specific website for further info you can open a URL for everyone. To end a meeting, select the Meeting drop down menu then select 'End Meeting.'

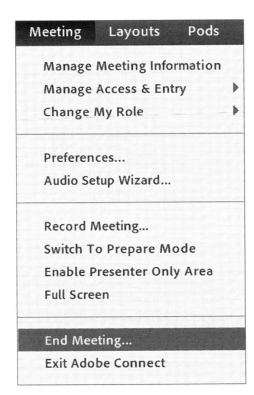

Note:
When a meeting is ended, all Attendees, including the host will be removed from the meeting room.

When a meeting has ended, all participants will be removed from the meeting.

Setting a Meeting End Message

Once you select 'End Meeting' to formally end a meeting, Adobe Connect will ask if you with to customize a message to all attendees. You can customize this message to say anything you want. When you select 'Save Message,' the meeting end message will be saved but you will be returned to the meeting without it ending.

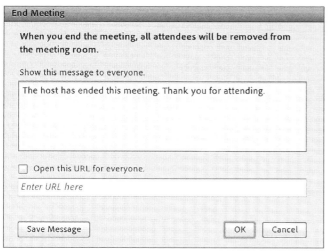

Custom messages when ending a meeting will be shown to all Attendees once OK is selected.

Quick Tip:
When selecting 'End Meeting' Adobe Connect allows you to populate an end of meeting message and URL without actually ending the meeting by selecting 'Save Message.'

Setting a URL to Sign-Off

When ending a meeting, Adobe Connect will allow you to add a URL and force all attendees to that website once the meeting is ended.

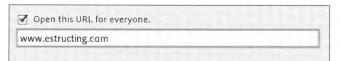

Forcing a URL is a great way to sent attendees to a specific website for further reading.

Reusing Your Meeting Room

Although a meeting room can be 'Ended,' once the meeting host re-enters the meeting room, a new 'session' of the meeting room will begin as Adobe Connect meeting rooms are persistent, and can be used over and over again.

Items to Reset

Before a meeting is used again for an additional session, it is best to reset a few pods in the meeting room.

1: Be sure to delete any unused pods (discussed in chapter 11.)

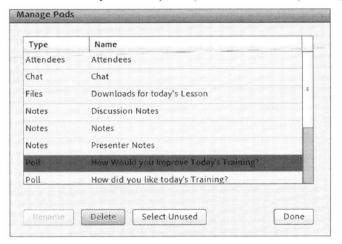

2: Be sure to clear the Chat pod (discussed in chapter 5.)

3: Reset the layouts to adjust the size of all pods back to the original default template (discussed in chapter 11.)

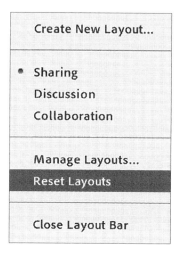

Quick Tip:
When managing the pods to reset a meeting room, be sure to not delete any pods you may want to re-open.

CHAPTER NOTES

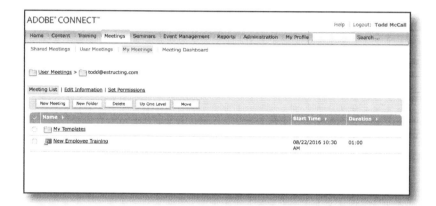

Overview:

Throughout this chapter, we will explore where all uploaded content is saved in Adobe Connect Central. We will also explore how to move, organize, upload and share content from the Adobe Connect server.

In This Chapter:

Note:
This chapter should take 30 minutes to explore all the aspects of the Content Tab.

Managing Content

Meeting Locations

When a meeting is first created by a meeting host, that meeting will go into the 'User Meetings' folder found inside Adobe Connect Central. Members of the 'Meeting Host' group receive their own folder to store meetings. If the meeting creator was not a member of the 'Meeting Hosts' group, that meeting will be placed into the 'Shared Meetings' folder.

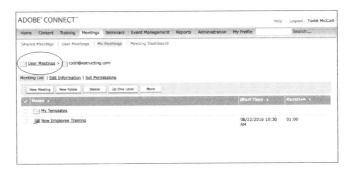

Adobe Connect User Meeting folder.

User Meeting Folders

Inside Adobe Connect Central, under the 'Meeting' Tab, Adobe Connect automatically directs the user to the 'My Meetings' folder, which is where all meetings created by that user are found. If a user is a member of the 'Administrator' group, they will have access to all user meeting folders as well as the 'Shared Meetings' folder.

Note:

As soon as a Meeting Host creates their first meeting, a User Meeting folder will be created for that user. This folder will not be removed if the user is removed from the Meeting Host group or deleted from t he system.

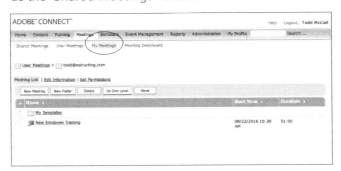

Adobe Connect 'My Meetings' list.

As an Administrator, when the 'User Meetings' tab is selected, it will list all of the past and present 'Meeting Host' folders.

Adobe Connect User Meetings folder.

Uploaded Meeting Content

During a meeting, all content shared gets saved onto the Adobe Connect server, more specifically, it is saved into a folder called 'Uploaded Content.' To access this folder inside Adobe Connect Central, select the 'Meetings' tab, then navigate to your meeting then select the sub-tab 'Uploaded Content.' Adobe Connect will list all the files ever shared in that meeting room.

Quick Tip:
Creating folders inside Adobe Connect Central is a best practice to keep your content organized

Adobe Connect meeting uploaded content list.

Organizing Your Content

All uploaded content can be moved to different locations such as 'Shared Content' or other user content folders. To move any uploaded meeting content, simply select the content you want to move and then select 'Move To Folder.'

Move To Folder button inside Adobe Connect Central.

Adobe Connect will prompt you to select a destination folder to which you can move your selected content.

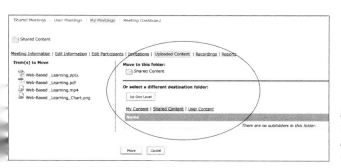

Destination location when moving content inside Adobe Connect Central.

Note:
All content stored in the 'Shared Content' folder can be accessed by all meeting hosts in all meetings.

Creating Content Folders

Adobe Connect Central will allow you to create sub-folders inside the user content folders and the shared content folders. This is a simple way to organize your content to be easily found during other meetings. To create a sub-folder, select the 'New Folder' button when inside any content folders.

New Folder button inside the Adobe Connect user content folder.

Pre-Loading Content

To upload content inside Adobe Connect Central, navigate to the upload destination folder and select the 'New Content' button, Adobe Connect will prompt you to name the content and give it a brief summary.

Note:
Only users that are members of the 'Administrator,' 'Meeting Host,' or 'Limited Administrator' groups can organize, or move content.

New Content button inside the Adobe Connect user content folder.

New content dialog box which asks to select, name, and summarize new content.

Loading User Content

During a meeting, hosts and presenters can access the user content and Shared content folders quickly and easily in the share content dialog box.

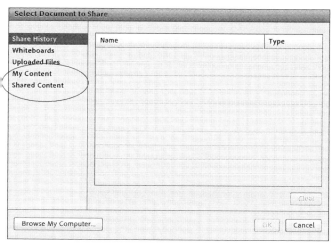

Quick Tip:
Uploading content directly to the Adobe Connect Central is a best practice to keep your content organized.

'My Content' and 'Shared Content' quick tabs found in the share content dialog box inside a Adobe Connect meeting.

CHAPTER NOTES

A

B

C

D

E

F

U

V

W

Pre-Meeting & Post-Meeting Checklist

Pre-Meeting

Pre-Meeting preparation is the key to a smooth and successful meeting. The following check list are items to consider before you begin your first live meeting:

* *Create your meeting room and prepare your layouts and pods.*
* *Pre-load meeting content/ presentations into appropriate pods.*
* *Prepare a Notes pod with housekeeping items - Teleconferencing numbers, reminder to mute mics*
* *Ensure you have the Adobe Connect "Add-In" installed should you require it for sharing your screen/ webcam during the meeting.*
* *Consider ahead of time what you're willing to share if screen sharing, whether it's your whole desktop, a single application, or a specific window and ensure no private content will be shared.*
* *Test your connection. (http://admin.adobeconnect.com/common/help/en/support/meeting_test.htm) to ensure your device meets the requirements*
* *Test your webcam, ensure that the Meeting room is finding the correct device should you have multiple.*
* *Test your Audio, whether your using VoIP (testing your microphone and speakers) OR Teleconferencing.*
* *Send a reminder email with the meeting room link to your participants so the link is readily available.*
* *Decide on the level of interaction you're looking to have with your participants and ensure meeting room rights have been allocated accordingly.*

Post-Meeting

After a meeting has concluded, check the following items to make the meeting room ready for future use:

* *End recordings.*
* *Close polls.*
* *Clear the Chat pod history.*
* *Reset layouts.*
* *Remove any documents from all Share pods that you will not use again.*
* *Turn off Microphone rights for participants.*
* *Turn off 'Auto Promote Participants to Presenters' if previously selected.*
* *Delete or rename any unwanted pods.*
* *In the Adobe Connect Central, delete or move any unwanted uploaded files*

Additional Training and Resources

Further Readings

For further reading on Adobe Connect, eStructing.com is offering 'Administrating Adobe Connect' (January 2017).

Topics discussed:

- *Integrating Your Audio (Teleconferencing)*
- *Meeting Attendance And Poll Reports*
- *Creating Custom Layouts*
- *Breakout Rooms*
- *Advanced Meeting Management – PAO, Prepare Mode*
- *Templates*
- *Creating An Connect Training Course*
- *Creating An Connect Training Curriculum*
- *Generating Connect Reports*
- *Creating An Connect Event*
- *Customizing Event Template*
- *Post Event Reports*
- *Managing Connect Users*
- *Customizing Your Connect Account*

Additional Training

For additional hands-on in-person or online training, New Toronto Group offers monthly Adobe Connect classroom training. Classes are offered in express one-day format for new users and three-day comprehensive classes for advanced users and Adobe Connect Administrators. For a complete listing of training classes, visit www.newyyz.com.

Resources

Adobe Connect offers a very extensive resource center with hundreds of tips from industry experts at https://www.connectusers.com. In Addition to Adobe Connect technical articles and updates, https://www. connectusers.com offers a full user forum to post questions and create discussion topics with industry professionals.

Inside 'Using Adobe Connect'

This workbook will assist both beginners and longtime, practiced, Adobe Connect professionals. As a Meeting Host you will be able to run effective, timesaving meetings. As more organizations and teams move toward a virtual environment, it is important that you establish and maintain a high level of interaction and collaboration. Adobe Connect and eStruct workbooks show you the tools to do just that, saving your organization time and money. **Chapters included:**

Adobe Connect Administration

Using Adobe Connect guides reader through the Adobe Connect Administration tab, creation of new users and groups, resetting passwords and understanding the different roles that users can be assigned in the Adobe Connect system.

Meeting Room Layout

Using Adobe Connect completely explores the Adobe Connect Meeting interface, all the menus and how to access various meeting features accessed during a web meeting.

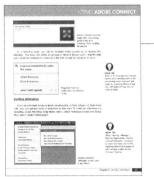

Managing Attendees

Using Adobe Connect explores how guests and registered users access the meeting room, how to place Participants on hold while you prepare your meeting and how to prevent users from accessing the meeting after it has begun.

41127256R00097

Made in the USA
Middletown, DE
08 March 2017